Behind the Mask:
Authentic Living
For Young Women

By Rebecca Bradley & Diane Roberts

Behind the Mask:
Authentic Living For Young Women

By Rebecca Bradley & Diane Roberts

featuring original artwork by Angela Hutson-Cumpston, godsgardenportraits.org

Behind the Mask Editor: Linda Dodge

Published by
Pure Desire Ministries International
P.O. Box 2310, Gresham, OR 97030
www.puredesire.org   503.489.0230

ISBN 978-0-9839993-2-4

First Printing February 2012

The stories of individual lives in this book are true and accurate. Some details have been adjusted to prevent personal identification. In some cases the story presented is a compilation of the histories of several individuals. The compilation, however, doesn't affect the clinical or theological veracity of the stories.

Behind the Mask:
Authentic Living for Young Women

Table of Contents

Acknowledgements

As Ted Roberts, founder of Pure Desire Ministries International, was writing the book *Top Gun, Flight Manual for Young Men in a Pornified World,* I began praying about a similarly focused book for young women. Soon, Rebecca Bradley entered my life. Becky is a high school science teacher who daily observed the hurt many girls face today. Her mentor Debora Nelson was instrumental in understanding what lies behind her own mask. This inspired her to invest into the lives of youth through writing. Getting to know the courageous young women in her girls' group motivated her to join me in writing this book. We offer thanks to these young women and other friends of Becky who were willing to share their stories with you—stories that reflect how horrific trauma cannot stop the fulfillment of God's promise of healing and restoration in their lives.

Becky extends special thanks to her husband Adam and daughter Hosanna Amya for the sacrifices they made to allow *Behind the Mask* to come to completion.

We are honored to include original artwork by Angela Hutson-Cumpston throughout this book. Having teen girls of her own, she, too, understands the necessity of reaching out to this next generation and wants to use her gifts to do just that. Please refer to Angela's website, godsgardenportraits.org, for more information about her art.

Adam Bradley, Lisa Fieldhouse and Joy Hekker were instrumental in designing the cover. Special thanks to Linda Dodge who spent hours editing and formatting this book; her heart for this project and creative eye has helped us put this book together in a timely fashion. We are also thankful for Bryan Roberts, the production manager over this project.

Finally, I want to thank the young women who volunteered to walk through this material as it was being created. They spent months processing and editing with us, giving valuable input into how *Behind the Mask* might match with the needs of their peers. To them we are extremely grateful.

Sincerely,

Diane Roberts, Co-founder
Pure Desire Ministries International

Introduction
Invitation to Face Reality

The more young women I meet, the more I realize that most are caught in the middle of a seemingly impossible task of reconciling who they want to be and who they are. They had goals, they had good intentions, but somewhere along the way they fell short of what they wanted out of life and who they wanted to become.

The mind of a young woman is shaped many years before she hits puberty. By six years of age, brain patterns are created that determine who to trust, where to find love, and how to get affirmation from others. Each life is set on a unique path based on environmental circumstances, family background, childhood abuse, stress in life growing up, genes, and basic instincts. These factors affect how you relate to others and behave sexually. Your story that began when you were born continues to shape you as you mature into adulthood.

Each of you has a unique story to tell. You have pictures in your mind of the mountains you have climbed, of your favorite moments on the top or the deep valleys on the bottom looking up. Much of your life is composed of quick snapshots along the way—painful, neutral, or compelling pictures that little by little shaped who you are.

If you did not get what you needed to feel safe, loved, and valued early in life, you probably have created masks or false identities that don't match with your inner self. Over time, the masks can define your identity and the person God created you to be gets covered up.

God knows you and He understands the story you have lived so far. He has plans ahead for you—good, good plans. He sees your bruises and scrapes. He already knows your insecurities; He can even see your inner heart and the pain you have faced over the years you have lived. He sees the masks you wear and He sees the hurt you are trying to avoid by presenting these masks to others. The amazing thing is that His strength and grace can heal the fearful parts of you so you can live in freedom without the facade. He can lead you down a new path to a life of freedom.

This book is written for young women struggling with wounds from the past that leave them vulnerable to unhealthy relational patterns, including compulsive sexual behavior. Processing through this book with a group of other young women will help you become aware of the life you have lived, take inventory of your present situation, and help you discern where healthy patterns of living can be developed, if you choose. Even though you may have pressures all around you and a world demanding your attention, we invite you to take some time to grow and heal with other young women who can share your curiosity, hopes, and fears.

We have gathered stories from young women all over the country who have survived abusive relationships and struggled through the toughest times in their lives to discover who they truly are and embrace all God created them to be. Their names have been changed to protect their privacy, but we assure you that the stories are true and the emotions accurate.

I (Rebecca) have personally struggled with love addiction and am learning to daily discipline my mind to accept the unconditional love of the Lord. Over the past eight years, I have worked with young women in church settings, helping them identify their fears, past abuse, and inner struggles. My experiences with *Just Be True* young women's group and conversations with my high school students have inspired me to co-write this book, which I hope will pave the way for healing in young women like you.

Diane is the wife of Dr. Ted Roberts, co-founder of Pure Desire Ministries International and the mother of two adult children. She regularly counsels women whose husbands struggle with sexual addiction, and also women struggling with love addiction and obsessive sexual behavior.

Artwork by Angela Hutson-Cumpston is featured in *Behind the Mask*. In hopes of expressing the intent of each lesson and the heart of God through it, Angela prayed over each drawing before creating it. We hope that you will experience the fullness of God's love and healing as you meditate on these drawings and complete the assignments within each lesson.

Our hope is that you will be able to live freely as you face your fears without the masks you have created. We pray that this book will help you learn how to meet your needs in healthy ways that allow you to trust God and let Him heal your heart.

Getting Started With *Behind the Mask*

Behind the Mask is designed for you to study alone or in a small group. You will receive more benefit if you can find a small group at your church or among your friends who are struggling with similar issues. All new beginnings are difficult, but knowing that you are not alone and that others are willing to join you in this adventure will give you hope.

Please read and sign the Memo of Understanding. We suggest that you sign this memo whether you are doing *Behind the Mask* in a group or on your own.

If you are using *Behind the Mask* with a group, please review the Small Group Guidelines and talk them over with your group so that everyone has a similar understanding about how the group will operate.

To enrich your *Behind the Mask* experience, we urge you to take time to respond to the questions integrated into each chapter and do other suggested activities, including journaling your thoughts on the song recommended at the end of each chapter. Deliberately participating in these mental exercises will help you counter the lies you have believed about yourself and your past.

Meet the first Behind the Mask Group! Desiring to remove their masks & become authentic, these young women processed each chapter, contributed ideas & provided creative feedback for the book as it was being written.

If you are a group leader, please consider ordering the *Behind the Mask Leader's Guide* with resources and suggestions that will assist you with creating and maintaining a safe and validating environment for the group participants. The *Leader's Guide* also includes ideas for presenting and discussing the information for many of the chapters.

Behind the Mask
Memo of Understanding for Group Participants

I understand that the facilitators and leaders will make every attempt to guard my anonymity and confidentiality as I participate in a *Behind the Mask* group. However, this cannot be absolutely guaranteed in a group setting.

- I realize that the group facilitator, leader or pastor cannot control the actions of others in the group.
- I realize that confidentiality is sometimes broken accidentally and without malice.

I understand that group leaders or facilitators are morally and ethically obligated to discuss with me any of the following behaviors that are observed, and that this may lead to the breaking of confidentiality and/or possibly intervention:

- I communicate an intention to harm myself.
- I communicate an intention to harm another person.
- I reveal ongoing sexual or physical abuse.
- I exhibit an impaired mental state.
- I reveal that I have perpetrated an act of child abuse and/or child molestation or have expressed the intent to commit such act.
- I reveal that I have perpetrated or am considering an abusive act toward the elderly and/or disabled.

I have been advised that the consequences for communicating the above types of information may include reports to the proper authorities—the police, suicide units or children's protective agencies, as well as to any potential victims. I further accept that if I am under the supervision of adult or youth authorities, part of my healing/recovery may include the need to notify those authorities.

I understand that *Behind the Mask* groups are Christ-centered groups that integrate healing tools with the Bible and prayer. I recognize that all members may not be of my particular church background or preference. I realize that the Bible may be discussed more or less than I would like it to be.

I understand that this is a support group and **not** a therapy group, and that the coordinator/leaders are qualified by life experience rather than by professional training as therapists. The facilitator or leader role in this group is to create a climate where healing may occur, to support my personal work towards recovery, and to share her own experience, strength and hope.

Name (please print) _____ **Date** _____

Group Participant Signature _____

Parent signature (if participant is a minor) _____

Behind the Mask **Group Leader Signature** _____

Pure Desire Ministries International 10/2011

Behind the Mask Group Guidelines

So that all group members will have the best possible experience, Pure Desire recommends the following guidelines.

Confidentiality is essential!
(What's said in the group is not shared outside the group.)

Speak only for yourself

Respect others
(Let everyone find her own answers/no side conversations.)

Limit sharing
(Everyone needs talking time!)

Start & end on time

Come prepared
(Review each lesson & take time to complete assignments)

Take responsibility
(If you feel uncomfortable with anything happening in the group or among group members, share your concern with the group or with the leader or co-leader.)

How to use the guidelines

- *Get agreement from the group: Can everyone agree to these guidelines?*
- *Add one or two more guidelines if needed as your group continues to meet. For example, to address cell phone/texting during class. Discuss, get agreement, add the guideline.*
- ***Post the guidelines during group time*** *so that are all reminded of agreed upon expectations from each other and the group.*
- *Review them when someone new joins the group.*

Chapter 1
The Masks We Wear

I have never been a fan of lying to my child. If it weren't for my husband, my toddler would already know Santa doesn't exist, that the tooth fairy is really just me, and that the Easter bunny doesn't really lay eggs. (My apologies to those of you whose bubbles I just burst.)

However, my daughter has this fascination with Strawberry Shortcake. Who would we invite to her third birthday but Strawberry Shortcake? My short, bubbly friend Ashley came dressed to impress at the party a few months ago. She was very convincingly dressed with the striped green and white stockings, white tutu under the pink dress, and the reddish hot pink hair wig. She had freckles painted on her face using eyeliner, fake eyelashes, and black shoes with straps. In spite of her façade, Ashley looked so genuine; the little girls flocked to her as she stepped into the party.

My daughter was a bit more hesitant than the other girls to buy into it. "I thought you had red shoes," she said after studying this real-life doll standing in her living room. Strawberry Shortcake looked surprised. "These are my party shoes!" she replied.

"What is your puppy and kitty's name?" my daughter quizzed her. Ashley looked at me with big eyes, "Ummm, they weren't able to come today," she replied, slyly avoiding the question. I glanced at a nearby poster of them. "Yes, honey," I said, "Pupcake and Custard probably had other things to do." Ashley mouthed the words *thank you* to me from across the room. "Pupcake and Custard don't like to travel," Ashley said. My daughter accepted that explanation as she jumped into the mountain of presents and allowed Strawberry to help her open the gifts.

I felt like the most deceiving person ever. Why would I try and get my own daughter to believe something that wasn't really true? Was I teaching her that deception is okay? I concluded that if this doesn't affect her ability to trust me, then it could possibly widen the scope of her imagination.

Either way, we can all get caught up in the use of **disguises**. Masks are convenient. They give us the illusion that they will keep us safe. Masks hide our insecurities and give us the false feeling that we are in control. They can even be impressive, concealing more than they project—such as our weaknesses, fears, insecurities, and loneliness. We painstakingly create what we think is a sophisticated facade in hopes of being accepted and loved, and hoping no one will discover what lies underneath.

The deep need for acceptance often drives us in the opposite direction of values we were raised with and have long believed. Low self-esteem drives us to seek satisfaction in unhealthy relationships that we mistakenly believe will bring happiness and show that we are in control. To fill our inner needs, we feel pressure to portray ourselves as young women we are not—whether online on social networking sites, online forums, or with a group of our peers.

Many young women have crossed sexual boundaries they thought they would never cross. Some have remained in abusive relationships, used sex to get love, or simply found it difficult to say "no" to sexual advances. According to a recent survey of high school students, 46 percent (freshmen through seniors) have had sexual intercourse[1], and more than half of teens ages 15 to 19 have engaged in oral sex.[2] The largest users of Internet porn are twelve to seventeen years old.[3] Nearly 75 percent of graduating high school students have had sex.[4] These statistics are evidence of a hurting population. These numbers can be discouraging for those wanting a lasting and faithful relationship.

Where does that leave you? The challenge to follow God without succumbing to the pressures to have sex before marriage is a difficult one. The combination of past trauma, society's values, and peer pressure makes the Christian walk and commitment very difficult.

You want to be accepted and at the same time you have emotional and physical drives going on within your body. Many times these feelings and desires begin pulling young women in a direction that is opposed to their commitment to Christ. In an age where you are discovering who you are and who you want to be, it is easy to try on different masks to feel accepted. You desire what God has for you, but you are pulled by overwhelming feelings that convince you that using your sexuality for acceptance is "so right." A desire for acceptance by church people, family, or other adults may increase the tension you already experience.

The pressure to survive in all these situations can move you to create a stash of different costumes you wear depending on who you are trying to impress: a school mask, a church mask, a home mask, and a mask you wear online. While trying to impress everyone around you, the true young woman you are may get lost in the muddle.

We want you to survive, but beyond that we desire for you to THRIVE with a heart for God, no matter what you have experienced. We want you to dive into the journey of knowing yourself as deeply as God does, loving yourself with grace, and facing life with an unexplainable anticipation for the future. As you travel through this book, you will have help to recognize your own masks and become aware of the pain behind them. Keep in mind that stopping destructive thought patterns and replacing them with life-giving patterns takes time. You are adventuring into a lifelong process of renewing your mind, changing how you think, and gaining the ability to become aware of your responses to life right now.

If you are struggling to be authentic and trying to walk in sexual integrity, you are not alone. Young women whose stories are shared in this book and other women around you have hidden behind the masks they created and crossed boundaries they have long held.

Unfortunately, many churches have used shame as a motivator to prevent girls from compromising their sexual integrity. In reality, this shame drives harmful lies deeper in young women's brains, causing more pain, leading to more need for love, which perpetuates seeking more unhealthy sexual encounters. The Bible accounts of Jesus' life indicate that He could identify women who were functioning in these patterns and He could see their motivation. Today, as for the women then, **He can see behind the mask.** He knows the pain, and He knows how to heal. No man you meet here on earth can do that for you.

If you have crossed the line sexually, like half the young women have, you will find hope. You are not a bad person. You are accepted just the way you are. You are loved no matter what you have done. God does not think anything less of you, and neither do we. Wherever you are in your journey, whether you have already crossed a line or not, sexual health and purity are still possible by the grace of God.

Being a true woman of God involves understanding who you are and who God is. A woman who knows her value will find inner strength and trust God with her relationships and her future. It IS possible in this turbulent, exciting, and challenging period of your life to become a true woman of God, equipped to love a man deeply and passionately all the days of your life. Yes, women like that are rare today. This book will help you to see you are not alone in this quest and that nothing worth living for is easy. You will not be told to "try harder" or "just stop it," as those approaches have never worked.

Instead, this book will give you some practical help on living smarter sexually. For you to be able to love your future husband with depth, you must realize the depth of God's love for you. The core of your sexual life is spiritual. In other words, your sexual health is directly related to your spiritual health. We are not talking about being religious or trying to perform for God. We are talking about the fact that **you are outrageously loved by God.** To fully discover this love, you will want to get together with other young women who also want God's best. This battle for walking in sexual purity cannot be won alone. Reading the chapters and then sharing your responses to the questions and exercises will not only strengthen you as an individual, but will also strengthen those in your group.

What is at stake?

Numerous Christian adults have trashed their marital relationship with their spouse and kids because of out-of-control sexual behavior. Perhaps you have seen this in your family or another family. Most did not receive healthy guidance before they were married and all brought unhealthy sexual patterns and expectations into the marriage. Whether you are struggling with love addiction, unhealthy sexual behaviors, or need new tools to live authentically, there is hope and there are answers.

We have teamed up with three other women who have experienced heartbreak similar to what you may have experienced. They lived behind their own masks until they began to pursue a healing journey that allowed them to unmask their lives. Their testimonies and insights, along with others, will inspire you to new heights in your walk with God and in your relationships with others.

Meet Jessica: *pleasing for love*

Always labeled the "good girl," Jessica tried everything she could to get people to like her. She thought that if she did everything right, God would love her and bless her. Coming from a home where sarcasm and criticism saturated everyday conversation, Jessica was petrified of doing anything wrong and being judged or rejected by her family. The concept that she could only gain love by meeting certain requirements was ingrained in her brain. Underneath her facade of having everything together, she ached for authentic relationship and unconditional love but led a life of anxiety, trying to follow all the rules. She desperately wanted a healthy relationship with guys, but hated herself so much because she felt she would never measure up. Too afraid to make a mistake, she avoided serious relationships lest she be rejected by a guy, her parents, her church, or God.

Meet Anna: *love at any cost*

Up until now, Anna was able to portray the healthy all-American girl to those around her. Now everyone—her Facebook friends, school friends, and even church friends—will see the truth. Underneath the confident and secure person she meticulously created was a girl with a heart broken from childhood trauma. In an attempt to fill the deep hurt from the past, she "used" a guy she hardly knew to gain attention. Anna stepped into a pattern of pleasing him by giving him whatever he asked, including messaging sexual content and nude pictures. Once things got too heated, she backed out of the relationship; then he forwarded the pictures to everyone he knew. His betrayal wounded her to the core. What would her friends, her church, and her parents think of her now? The facade that protected her was gone. So was her reputation. She was crushed.

Sisters of the Heart
By Angela Hutson-Cumpston

Meet Cindy: *validation through sex*

Cindy was the girl everyone wanted to be around. Her pretty face and figure attracted the guys' attention, her kind heart won over the females in her life, and her love for Jesus pleased those at church. Outwardly she was confident, happy, and sensual. Somehow she could get away with wearing skimpy clothing and not looking like a whore. She seemed to have it all. She was happy to party on the weekend and just as content to praise God at youth group. Inwardly she was a little girl with a deep, deep desire to be held by her daddy. Her father had been absent when she was a child and had committed suicide when Cindy was in elementary school. Following God's best for her life was much harder when she met her boyfriend and he moved into the basement of a friend's house. Suddenly they had an unlimited access to express the passion that raged under their skin. Keeping her boundaries became more and more difficult, and guilt grew in her heart the further she strayed from her boundaries.

Meet You!

☙ **How do you relate to any of these young women?**

_____

_____

_____

☙ **Write a short excerpt of your story right now, explaining one challenge that you are presently facing or have recently faced.**

_____

_____

_____

_____

_____

_____

_____

_____

_____

_____

_____

_____

_____

_____

_____

_____

_____

_____

_____

Which of these masks do you think Jessica, Anna and Cindy wore?

- Write the letter **J** next to those that might apply to Jessica.
- Write the letter **A** next to those that apply to Anna.
- Write the letter **C** next to those that might reflect Cindy.

J (Jessica) A (Anna) C (Cindy)	Mask	Distorted Beliefs
	Self-sufficient mask	People may need me but I don't need anyone.
	Fortress mask	Protects me from getting close to people who could hurt me.
	Take Charge mask	I have to be in control so I won't get hurt.
	Superior mask	If I look better than others I will be accepted
	Victim's mask	Everyone is trying to hurt me.
	Party mask	I have to be the life of the party to be accepted.
	Pleaser mask	I can't say "no" because I will be liked if I am needed.
	Vanity mask	My value comes from my outward appearance.
	Rescuer mask	I am responsible for others' problems, feelings or behaviors.
	Performance mask	My value is based on my performance & how well I measure up.
	Happy mask	People only like me when I am happy & fun to be with.
	"I Can Do It" mask	Asking for help is a sign of weakness.
	Perfectionist mask	I won't be liked if I make mistakes.
	Rebel mask	I'm part of the crowd when I go against my values.
	Flirtatious mask	I must be pursued to prove I have value.

We all wear masks because we fear the rejection we believe will come if people really knew us or knew what has happened to us. List the masks that you have used to protect yourself in the past and in the present:

_____

_____

_____

_____

_____

_____

∜ **What have you experienced as a result of wearing these masks?**

_____

_____

_____

_____

_____

∜ **How have they helped or hindered your life?**

_____

_____

_____

_____

_____

_____

Why did these young women feel the need to wear all those masks? Going back to the origin of mask wearing can give us some clues. It all started in the garden when God asked Adam, "Where are you?" God asks questions hoping we will figure out what is going on.

Adam's response is, *"I heard you in the garden and I was afraid because I was naked. And I hid."* (Genesis 3:10 MSG)

Adam and Eve fashioned the first masks out of leaves in an attempt to hide their shame, embarrassment, and fear over what they had done. Masks can also be fashioned to cover what others have done to us, as in the case of the women you read about who suffered abuse.

Why are we so quick to reach for masks? Elaborate masks are created to cover and to project an illusion that protects us from our fears and shame. The problem is that once the mask is on, it becomes difficult to take it off. We begin to deceive ourselves, assuming this is who we really are. In reality, most others can see right through the masks.

Not only do masks take a lot of energy to maintain, but also they literally suffocate the beauty of who God created us to be. There is an inability to discover our uniqueness because we try to be someone we are not. The very parts of us we are trying to hide—those weaknesses, shortcomings, hurts, and sins—are the very places God wants to do His next miracles. The Apostle Paul, in his New Testament letters to the early Christian church, often talked about his own weaknesses. In 2 Corinthians 12: 9-10 he declares God wanted to bring strength to his life at those very places of weakness.

The very thing we are desperately seeking—unconditional love and acceptance—actually becomes unattainable when we put on masks. The feelings of emptiness continue because only the mask receives the love. Deep down we feel the fear of "if they knew the real me they wouldn't love or accept me."

Keep your eyes open this week as you observe the masks that people in your life use to cover up their insecurities. Try to identify times when your feelings on the inside do not match up with what you are expressing on the outside. When you can distinguish the duplicity in yourself, you can intentionally allow the Lord to speak His unconditional grace into the damaged parts of your heart.

  ❧ **In the space below, journal the masks you identify during the week, worn by yourself and others. Circle the masks you identify as ones you wore this week.**

_____

_____

_____

_____

_____

_____

_____

_____

_____

_____

_____

Song recommendation for meditation this week:
A More Beautiful You
by Jonny Diaz

Chapter 2
Unmasking God's Grace

Anna: *love at any cost*

I met Anna at church camp. Beautiful girl, has the whole world ahead of her. She wore dark makeup around her eyes and kept her long hair pulled back in a tight ponytail. Even though she was shorter than many other 14-year-old girls, she made up for her height in strength and speed. She could always keep up with the guys on the game field. She seemed pretty shy when we first met, but we soon became inseparable friends. One warm night we were tucked into our bunk beds and spilling our secrets, and Anna had the courage to open up and tell me her story.

At a young age, Anna had been sexually abused multiple times. I mention this fact not because it defines who she is, but because she was shaped by it; many of the deepest issues she faces stem back to those fearful nights. She was raped by her mother's boyfriend, and she had kept what happened to her a secret.

Going into her teen years, sweet Anna was loyal to her boyfriend, even when he asked her to do things that made her feel uncomfortable. He asked her to text nude photos of herself to him and she complied. He promised not to tell anyone. She told him her darkest struggles and shared with him the abuse she had faced. He was supposed to be a Christian kid, she trusted him, and wanted to be close to him. This boy kept pressing for more and more sexual encounters with her and she was unwilling to give him more. Their relationship ended after he told his friends about her sexual abuse. Anna struggled with friend groups during sixth and seventh grade; by her eighth grade year, she escaped the shame by enrolling in a school in a different town where no one knew her. Her move changed her environment but didn't change the patterns embedded in her life. Anna met new friends, but they were also involved with guys. She met another guy and, for the sake of saving the relationship, she also texted him nude photos of herself. Even though she knew it was wrong, it was almost as if she couldn't help herself.

The night I met Anna at camp, her tears flowed as she looked at her past and grieved the choices she had made. She confessed that she was doing what she didn't want to do and not doing what she wanted to do. Anna was letting guys control her actions; she knew her relationships were unhealthy, but felt she couldn't change. If life were ideal for Anna, she would feel safe in her own skin, be herself, and not live under the fear of men. She felt alone, controlled, and hopeless for a better future for herself.

Cindy: *validation through sex*

Cindy, a fun-loving and beautiful girl, met Luke a few months into her junior year of high school, when she was 17. When Cindy first saw him, she thought he would be a fun guy for making out, going to parties, and going to dances, but never thought anything serious would become of it.

While putting on the flirty charm, she won his affection and they started dating. There was one problem—he wouldn't kiss her! Luke had kissed other girls, but he really liked Cindy and didn't want to mess it up. Cindy thought it was so sweet that he would pursue her like that. A few months into their relationship he took her to a park, swung her on the swings and kissed her. It was a great first kiss. She went home dreaming about his lips, yearning for the moment they would spend more time together. Right after that, he moved from his parents' house into a guy friend's house. Cindy and Luke began spending a lot of time in his basement with the lights off, watching movies or hanging out. Their physical relationship escalated more quickly than she had anticipated. What started as making out turned to messing around, touching each other, and soon they ended up on the couch almost naked. After that, the trips to the basement involved what they called "experimenting." She admits now that it was sex, but at the time, she and Luke gave other names to what they were doing so she wouldn't feel bad about it afterwards. In her mind, if she did everything except have intercourse then she could still keep her "good girl" mask.

After that, it felt so good to her that they moved on from "experimenting" and ended up having unprotected sex for an entire year. It was a miracle she didn't get pregnant. Cindy didn't tell anyone what she was doing. She and Luke became very secluded within themselves, but she kept going to church and youth group. She felt guilty every time they had sex without being married, but the guilt made her want sex even more to ease the pain of her hurt inside. It was a vicious, unforgiving cycle.

Her mind, heart, and body were intertwined with his. When her senior year came around, Cindy started feeling that Luke didn't want to be with her. He was hanging around with his guy friends more and all of her friends were choosing whether or not to go to college. It was a time of making huge, life-changing decisions. She didn't know if he was the guy she was going to be with for the rest of her life, but she felt so bonded with him that it was hard to imagine being with anyone else. Over time, Cindy began to notice that her emotional relationship with Luke didn't add up to what they had physically. She felt like she was playing the part of a girlfriend, but not really having the intimate relationship of her dreams.

Anna and Cindy are not alone. In counseling young women over the years, several things have become glaringly apparent. First of all, the spiritual battle for sexual health has reached new levels of intensity. Secondly, more trauma in the lives of young people has created the need for more masks to cope with the deep wounds in their minds. This trauma creates patterns or roadways in the brain that are directly related to sexuality. The combination of trauma, heightened peer pressure, and advancing technology has propelled more young people to engage in sexual behavior at earlier ages. You are growing up in an overly sexualized culture that is full of pain.

If you have crossed the line with boundaries you have set or if you have done things you never planned on doing, you are not alone. Read the statistics below. Do you see yourself in any of them? "Teen girls" indicate those who are ages 13 to 19 years old; "young adults" are categorized as those 20 to 26[5].

- **22% of teen girls and 36% of young adult women have sent or posted nude or semi-nude pictures or videos of themselves.**

- **37% of teen girls and 56% of young adult women have sent or posted sexually suggestive messages to others.**

- **51% of teen girls say pressure from a guy is why girls send sexy messages or images.**

- **23% of teen girls say they were pressured by friends to send or post sexual content.**

- **Among the women who have sent sexually suggestive content, 66% of teens and 72% of young adult women say they do so to be "fun or flirtatious."**

Sadly, those who posted sexually suggestive messages naively thought such messages would remain private. The reality is **40% of teens and young adults say they have had a sexually suggestive message (originally meant to be private) shown to them**[6].

In this same survey, **29% of teen boys agreed that girls who send such content are expecting to date or hook-up in real life**.

It may be easier to be provocative online, but whatever you text or post contributes to the real life impression you are making.[7]

☞ **In which statistics do you see yourself or some of your friends?**

_____

_____

_____

☞ **Why do young women engage in sexual activity? Below are some answers from other young women. Circle the reasons that tempt you most:**

to feel loved   gain acceptance   curiosity   peer pressure   hormones   ipods

because someone else did   to keep a boyfriend   drug & alcohol influence

rebellion   media pressure—porn   Internet   cellphones

other _____

☞ **What kinds of peer pressure have you experienced?**

_____

Are you ready for some good news? **God STILL loves and accepts you regardless of past choices.** He sees behind the mask you wear. He knows that the society in which you have been raised is becoming increasingly dark. But, just as the light shines in the darkness, God's grace can now be seen as never before. Even if you have made choices like Anna or Cindy, this does not make you damaged goods. God doesn't measure us according to how perfectly we live, but He does want to heal and restore areas of hurt and places you feel damaged.

You may have crossed the line sexually, as have many of the young women I have counseled. You may feel you can't go to your parents or anyone at church. However, by working through this book, you are declaring you are willing to learn how to fight and win with confidence, competence, and courage.

It is usually in dark, pressure-filled times that God does His best work. Therefore, you are in a perfect situation for God, through the work of the Holy Spirit, to take your struggles and sexuality and use them to shape you into the woman He had in mind when He first created you.

Anna was never created to be abused. Cindy was never designed to be squeezed into a mold of sexuality and live fearfully behind a mask. She was not meant to be trapped in a relationship out of guilt. Each young woman was created to become the unique individual God says she is to be.

The masks of these women have helped them handle the pain of their past trauma, but the day has come for each to face what is behind that mask, address the lies she has believed her entire life, and ponder anew who God says she is. The same goes for you. You were not made to be abused. You were never designed to fit into a box that someone else made for you, but rather to become uniquely who God says you are. Paul underlines this in Scripture: *Don't copy the behavior and customs of this world, but be a new and different person with a fresh **newness in all you do and think**. Then you will learn from your own experience how his ways will really satisfy you.* (Romans 12:2 Living Bible)

Paul draws a masterful contrast between being a copycat of the world and being a new and different person who doesn't have to imitate others. To copy the world means assuming an outward expression that doesn't come from within.[8] You might feel shame over your sexual struggles because **you are substituting short-term intensity for genuine intimacy**. Once shame takes root in your soul, it becomes a major driver for further sexual bondage. The only way out is coming to a "new in all you do and think" perspective.

Many times, "becoming new" is interpreted in the church setting as doing everything else that the other church people are doing: listening to Christian music, wearing Christian clothing, etc. In reality, this is still copying someone else, just under a Christian name. You do not have to try harder to be someone else or try harder to become more religious! Religion is a one-way communication with God where you are trying to please Him. Authentic Christianity is about a two-way communication where you are hearing Him speak of His unconditional love for you on a daily basis.

Let's continue to look at the story of Jessica, a young woman who struggled to believe that God could love her with no strings attached.

Jessica: *pleasing for love*

Jessica had the same dissatisfaction with her life as Cindy and Anna, but had a completely different lifestyle. President of the National Honor Society, Jessica got nothing but straight A's in school and had friends from church that she enjoyed hanging out with. On the outside was a girl who seemed to be successful, but inwardly under the mask of perfection, Jessica was being torn apart little by little, day by day.

Despite her exceptional grades, Jessica's looks were anything but exceptional. She had the kind of looks that were cute on a little girl, but not the type of beauty that her peers seemed to have grown into after middle school. No makeup, no highlights in her hair, no mascara highlighting her eyes. She couldn't use her parents' money to buy clothes without her mother's approval, which resulted in her wardrobe consisting of shirts a size too large, baggy jeans and sports bras from Walmart. She remembered how her mother had cried when she, at 13, had ventured to highlight her hair by herself; she remembered how guilty she had felt for doing something that made her mom sad.

For as long as she could remember, her mom had always said that beauty was found on the inside, and told Jessica she was "naturally" beautiful on the inside and out. Jessica never believed it. Instead, she interpreted these instructions as warnings that her parents would reject her if she presented herself in a way other than "natural." She knew her dad disapproved of makeup, so she had never learned what makeup to buy or how girls made it look so great. Though envious of others, she tended to criticize those who used it.

Highlighting her hair wasn't the first time that her mom had cried over a choice Jessica made on her own. In eighth grade, Jessica had said "yes" when a boy had asked her to go out with him. When Jessica's mom overheard her talking to the guy on the phone, Jessica told her she was talking with her boyfriend; her mom left the room sobbing that her "little girl" (then 14) was growing up. Feeling guilty over a "bad" choice that hurt her mom and feeling like a failure in her parents' eyes, Jess dumped the guy the next day and swore off dating until she was 16, the rule that her parents had now drawn in stone.

As a middle school student, Jessica's favorite thing to do had been to sink her mind into *Seventeen* magazines that other girls brought to school. What her parents had called forbidden, Jess called delicious. When her dad found out she was reading teen magazines, he took them away from her, saying, "You can read that when you are seventeen." Afterwards, Jessica fell into deep guilt and regret for betraying her family values. She couldn't deny the feeling that her parents wouldn't let her grow up; she felt stuck at age 12. For Jessica's fifteenth birthday, her mom made a "Barbie" cake. While other girls were going to underage dance clubs for their birthdays, Jess had hers at a mini-golf course, supervised by her parents.

She knew there was more to high school than getting good grades and the constant quest to measure up and gain approval, but she couldn't stop herself from trying. The thought began to eat away at her heart incessantly. Jessica and her mom were constantly on edge. Anything her mom said seemed an attempt to invade her life and to change her into someone her mom wanted her to be.

She was so done with feeling controlled by her parents, but too afraid to rebel. If she had rebelled, she felt she would lose her parents' love. Instead, she lived her entire high school years anxiously walking on the tightrope, trying to please her parents without falling off into the unknown. At the same time, she was enclosed within the dreams and conditions of her parents and felt incapable of making her own decisions. Jessica's face got used to the mask of perfection she put on every morning. It seemed to be a permanent mold she lived behind. Her parents' thoughts became her own. Jessica didn't know who she was. Every thought, every action was seeped through the filter of "What would my parents think?"

Any time Jessica tried to live her own life, the choices were followed with such incredible guilt that she tortured herself with shameful thoughts such as, "I will never be good enough." She had zero self-confidence and had trouble making even small decisions on her own. She raged inside with a desire to live freely, but the fear inside her to please her parents drove her instincts the exact opposite direction. Jessica was doing what she didn't want to do—letting them live her life for her; she was not doing what she wanted to do—be herself, stop living in anxiety of what people think of her, and make adult decisions in a healthy way.

What does God think?

God is not obsessed with what you do. In fact, He gives us freedom to make mistakes. God is not obsessed with your sin, either. He dealt with your sin past, present, and future at the cross. He sees those areas where you have fallen or struggled sexually as opportunities to bring healing and change into your life.

☙ **What opportunity for God's healing do you see in your own life?**

The **Love Addiction Evaluation** that follows can help give you clarity as to where God may want to do His next miracle. Answer the statements honestly in light of your present struggles.

LOVE ADDICTION EVALUATION[9]

☙ **Put a check next to any statements that describe you in the present or have described you in the past.**

_____ 1. I am driven by one or more compulsions (relationships, sex, food, drugs, etc.).

_____ 2. I think my self-esteem is low.

_____ 3. I think that my happiness depends on having a loving relationship.

_____ 4. I often fantasize to avoid reality or loneliness.

_____ 5. I feel I need to be "good" enough to earn love from others.

_____ 6. I will do almost anything for that desired loving relationship.

_____ 7. I find it difficult to say "no" and set healthy boundaries, especially with men.

_____ 8. I keep looking for a relationship to fill what is missing or lacking in my life.

_____ 9. I find myself thinking that things will (or would) be better in this new relationship.

_____ 10. I have always felt a distance and/or lack of love from my mom or dad.

_____ 11. I have a difficult time having an intimate relationship with God.

_____ 12. I vacillate from over-control to out-of-control behavior in any of these areas: relationships, sex, food, money, drugs.

_____ 13. I crave and fear intimacy at the same time.

_____ 14. I have used sex to get love.

_____ 15. I have used sex and seduction to dominate a man and be in control.

_____ 16. I take responsibility for people, tasks and situations for which I am not responsible.

_____ 17. I find myself in relationships that echo my past abuse.

_____ 18. I was sexually abused as a child or adolescent.

_____ 19. I have stayed in romantic relationships after they became emotionally or physically abusive.

_____ 20. I often find myself preoccupied with sexual thoughts or romantic daydreams.

_____ 21. I do have trouble stopping my sexual behavior when I know it is inappropriate.

_____ 22. I have hurt others emotionally because of my sexual/romantic behavior.

_____ 23. I do feel bad at times about my sexual behavior.

_____ 24. I have worried about people finding out about my sexual activities.

_____ 25. I feel controlled by my sexual desire or fantasies of romance.

_____ 26. I have been sexually or romantically involved with inappropriate people, such as a boss or a married person.

_____ 27. When I have sex or am involved in sexual activity, I often feel depressed afterwards.

_____ 28. I have become emotionally or sexually involved with people I don't know.

❧ **Review your responses and add up the total number of items you checked.**

_____ **Total number of items checked.**

If you scored over 3 (or more) in this evaluation, God's response is always, "That is where I want to do my next miracle."   Want evidence of that?

Look at Jesus' response to the woman at the well in John Chapter 4.

> [4] *He had to go through Samaria on the way.* [5] *Eventually he came to the Samaritan village of Sychar, near the field that Jacob gave to his son Joseph.* [6] *Jacob's well was there; and Jesus, tired from the long walk, sat wearily beside the well about noontime.* [7] *Soon a Samaritan woman came to draw water, and Jesus said to her, "Please give me a drink."* [8] *He was alone at the time because his disciples had gone into the village to buy some food.*
>
> [9] *The woman was surprised, for Jews refuse to have anything to do with Samaritans. She said to Jesus, "You are a Jew, and I am a Samaritan woman. Why are you asking me for a drink?"*
>
> [10] *Jesus replied, "If you only knew the gift God has for you and who you are speaking to, you would ask me, and I would give you living water."*
>
> [11] *"But sir, you don't have a rope or a bucket," she said, "and this well is very deep. Where would you get this living water?* [12] *And besides, do you think you're greater than our ancestor Jacob, who gave us this well? How can you offer better water than he and his sons and his animals enjoyed?"*
>
> [13] *Jesus replied, "Anyone who drinks this water will soon become thirsty again.* [14] *But those who drink the water I give will never be thirsty again. It becomes a fresh, bubbling spring within them, giving them eternal life."*
>
> [15] *"Please, sir," the woman said, "give me this water! Then I'll never be thirsty again, and I won't have to come here to get water."*
>
> [16] *"Go and get your husband," Jesus told her.*
>
> [17] *"I don't have a husband," the woman replied.*
>
> *Jesus said, "You're right! You don't have a husband—* [18] *for you have had five husbands, and you aren't even married to the man you're living with now. You certainly spoke the truth!"*

John 4: 4-18 (NLT)

The woman at the well was a classic love addict. In Jesus' time, a woman would be an outcast if she had been married five times and was living with a man to whom she wasn't married. Women in a hot desert culture would normally go to the well early in the morning or in the cool of the evening. There was so much shame attached to her lifestyle that she went to the well at noon to draw water. Scripture tells us Jesus was intentional about His journey through Samaria. Most Jews and Rabbis would never go through this geographical area, but Jesus had a divine appointment. He knew this woman would have answered "yes" to many of the questions on the Love Addiction Evaluation.

The following are statements she would have checked as being true in her life:

#3. I think my happiness depends on having a loving relationship.
#7. I find it difficult to say "no" and set healthy boundaries, especially with men.
#8. I keep looking for a relationship to fill what is missing or lacking in my life.
#9. I find myself thinking that things will (or would) be better in this new relationship.
#14. I have used sex to get love.
#23. I feel bad at times about my sexual behavior.
#24. I have worried about people finding out about my sexual activities.

  To which statements in the Love Addiction Evaluation can you most relate?

_____

_____

_____

  Circle one or two that you would feel comfortable sharing with your small group.

  Give an example of how one or more of these statements is true for you.

_____

_____

_____

_____

  Highlight the segments in the following definition of Love Addiction with which you can most identify.

> The Love Addict makes love and relationships the focus of her pursuit. Having a relationship can give her a false sense of feeling secure, accepted and valued. She desperately wants to satisfy the deep desire to belong. Relationships become a way of avoiding and even medicating the pain in her life. Love is pursued at all cost. Many times the price turns into a compromise of moral values where she will pursue one relationship after another in trying to fill the emptiness in her life.

Ladies, we are made to love God and love people deeply with our hearts. Love is good. Sex is good. In fact, God made us for both.   He said in Ecclesiastes 9:9 (NLT):

Live happily with the woman you love through all the meaningless days of life that God has given you under the sun. The wife God gives you is your reward for all your earthly toil.

When we believe lies about ourselves or have had abuse in our development, the gift of sex and love that God has given us can be distorted. When we use sex to medicate our pain, we create coping patterns that are difficult to break. Eventually, a woman can lose her identity and ability to communicate honestly. She may become an empty shell living behind the mask of sex or love to find validation.

You may have felt uncomfortable answering the evaluation and some of the questions in this lesson. You are not alone. Notice how the woman at the well put on the spiritual mask when she became uncomfortable with Jesus' questions about her personal life:

[19] *"Sir," the woman said, "you must be a prophet.* [20] *So tell me, why is it that you Jews insist that Jerusalem is the only place of worship, while we Samaritans claim it is here at Mount Gerizim, where our ancestors worshiped?"*

[21] *Jesus replied, "Believe me, dear woman, the time is coming when it will no longer matter whether you worship the Father on this mountain or in Jerusalem.* [22] *You Samaritans know very little about the one you worship, while we Jews know all about him, for salvation comes through the Jews.* [23] *But the time is coming— indeed it's here now—when true worshipers will worship the Father in spirit and in truth. The Father is looking for those who will worship him that way.* [24] *For God is Spirit, so those who worship him must worship in spirit and in truth."*

[25] *The woman said, "I know the Messiah is coming—the one who is called Christ. When he comes, he will explain everything to us."*

[26] *Then Jesus told her, "I AM the Messiah!"*

John 4: 19-26 (NLT)

We, like this woman, can spend a lot of time trying to avoid reality by hiding behind masks because the shame level is so high. One side effect is that it keeps us in a constant state of denial. In order to stop the unwanted behavior of our past, we must begin breaking through the denial structures in our brain that protect, excuse, and justify unhealthy patterns.

Some of the justifications we use to secure our masks are listed below.

<u>Spiritualize:</u> Twisting Scripture to justify our behavior.

Examples
- *It doesn't say anything in Scripture about masturbation.*
- *God wouldn't want me to be alone.*
- *We committed our relationship to one another before God; we don't need a piece of paper.*
- *I've been hurt by past relationships; I'm just looking for my soul mate now.*
- *He's a Christian, so it must be right.*

<u>Minimize:</u> Admitting there is a problem but minimizing its importance; comparing your problem to the problems of others and thinking, "My problems are nothing compared to _____."

Examples
- *We're only experimenting (Cindy's excuse).*

- *I only masturbate when I am stressed.*
- *Oral sex isn't really sex.*
- *We keep our clothes on while we pleasure each other.*
- *I just drink a little to take the edge off while we mess around.*
- *I send suggestive messages, but haven't sent any nude pictures like my friends.*
- *It's only online. It's not real sex.*
- *Masturbation is OK if we mutually masturbate each other.*

Blame: Finding fault with other people or situations rather than taking personal responsibility.

Examples
- *My friends were pressuring me to send nude photos.*
- *My boyfriend said he would dump me if I didn't "put out" sexually.*
- *My parents wouldn't let me date him, so I had to lie and sneak around to see him.*
- *My parents won't let me date, so I have started "messing around" with some of my girlfriends.*
- *No one understands me like he does.*
- *Everyone else is doing it.*

Rationalizing: Using excuses or justification for your behavior or the behavior of others who have hurt you.

Examples
- *I drank too much and couldn't say "no."*
- *My friends have gone all the way; we are just doing oral sex.*
- *I am lonely, and sexting helps me feel wanted.*
- *I am lonely, so I need a guy to fill that void.*

✌ What justifications have you used? Use the chart that follows for the next exercise.

1. List the justification and reasons you have used to rationalize your behavior.
2. Next, do the hard part! Break through the denial by listing the painful truth about your justification and behavior.

Justification/Truth Table

Justification/Denial structure	The truth about the justification of your behavior
Example: *I am lonely, and I need a guy in my life.*	*I do feel lonely, but I want a guy to accept me so that I can accept myself. Truth is that God accepts me all the time no matter what.*
1.	
2.	
3.	

You may have had a difficult time writing in the "truth" part of the chart; that is a normal response. You may have been so focused on rationalizing or minimizing your behavior that the truth has been hard to recognize. And you, like other young women, may not know what the truth is. Perhaps you have never had an example in your life of a healthy relationship. Keep pressing on and processing through this work! New experiences are ahead!

Finally, we want to underline that no matter how you scored on the Love Addiction Evaluation, **Jesus is 100% for you**. As mentioned before, He is excited to do His next miracle at the point of your most hidden and shame-filled places.

As you may remember from the beginning of this chapter, Anna was involved in unhealthy relationships and felt there was no way out. In eighth grade, she discovered a safe group of people she could talk to about her pain, and she met a loving God for the first time. This was the beginning of a healing process that would be long and arduous, but would give her tools to help her see her true self and hear God speak of His love for her daily.

Just like Anna, you, too, can experience that love and have a personal relationship with Jesus. Maybe you are ready to say "Yes" to Jesus or you realize you need to renew that commitment. If you are ready, pray this simple prayer and then share your decision with your group.

Dear God, I need You in my life. I am thankful that Jesus died on the cross to forgive me of all my sins past, present and future. I now invite You, Jesus, into the rooms of my life that have been hidden, and the places where I have struggled. I ask that you would come into my life as my Savior and Lord, and that You would show me how to live in healthy ways. Lord, help me accept Your love and understand You have a purpose for my life.

This is just the beginning, ladies. You have begun a process of new experiences that will rewire the damaged thought patterns in your mind and take you to a place of reality, health and fullness. Take heart!

> **Song recommendation for meditation this week:**
> ## *You Are More*
> ### by Tenth Avenue North

Playing with Fire

Chapter 3
The Disguised Cost of Dangerous Pursuits

A male friend of ours just got engaged; he had been living with the girl for a year. They have already given themselves to each other sexually and are not shy to admit it. Have they followed what God outlined as a healthy relationship? No. Does God still love them? Most definitely a resounding "YES!" And me? I am overjoyed at the proposal and am super excited for their future marriage.

So, if God still loves them and family is still excited, then what has been lost? What are the consequences, if any, to their less than prudent sexual relationship? In this chapter you will read stories of women who have varied experiences within their sexual relationships. You will be offered an honest look at how life has unfolded for these women. We will conclude with an opportunity for you to explore your own life and patterns of thought that affect how you relate to yourself and others.

In ancient Bible times the marriage celebration lasted an entire week. The real party began after the couple had consummated the marriage by having sex. You see, having sex was the evidence of a covenant commitment between a man and a woman. Even now, a man or woman can legally get his or her marriage contract annulled if they have not had sex. There is something about sex that is legally binding or not binding in court. We have these values after marriage, but where does that leave sex before marriage? What happens if the evidence of marriage (sex) comes before the wedding, where the covenant relationship has been established? Media often portray that the opposite is normal; in many plotlines, sex occurs before the couple has even professed their love for each other, much less had a covenant relationship established.

Are my friend and his girlfriend already technically married because they have had sex? If that were the case, why would I still be filled with butterflies and great hopes for their wedding day? I find my answer in looking behind the purpose of marriage.

When two people join together sexually within marriage, they reflect the image of God's oneness. Genesis 2:26 (NKJ) says, *"Let us make man in our image, according to our likeness."* God came up with the idea of marriage so we could experience some of the oneness reflected in God. It makes sense that God would want us to experience that closeness with someone who was covenantally committed to us. Sex outside of marriage simply falls short of what God intended.

 ❧ **Contrast what was stated about a marriage covenant commitment to the opinions of some of your peers or society in general.**

_____

_____

_____

Is a person better or worse for having or not having sex outside of marriage? Let's see what Cindy says from her experience

Cindy: "Never try to get validation from sex; you will always feel awful about it."

Cindy realized as she was sleeping with her boyfriend that she was doing this to validate her own feelings of insufficiency. If she had a bad day or had stressful circumstances, Cindy would always go to Luke in order to feel better about herself. And she would. She would feel wonderfully loved and accepted for moments, but afterward always felt bad about it. A deep, sinking feeling in her stomach would remind her that this was only outward acceptance, not the kind of security and inward acceptance she needed. Cindy tried to find her security in her boyfriend, but to him, sex was just a release and not a commitment to something further. To add to the shame, she had to hide it from her family, fearful that if they found out they would not accept her. Her escalating sex life set her up for broken relationships within her family, her friends, and with God. Further, she isolated herself, leaving her feeling like damaged goods. Now she can see where those patterns have gotten her. She says now, "Never get your validation from sex; you will always feel awful about it!"

"Once I understood that God wants what is best for me, I could see how my actions were affecting my relationship with Him. God isn't legalistic; He gives us rules because He knows that if we break these rules, our hearts will be broken, ripped out of our chest. No loving parent would wish that upon their daughter. Now that I am a mom, I understand. As a mom I can see a car coming down a street before my daughter crosses the road and yell, "Stop! Look both ways!" God's warnings function the same way; they are intended to prevent pain because He knows my body and heart. When I sought validation through sex outside of marriage, I had deep hurts on the inside. Of course He did not want my heart to be broken; it hurts His heart to see mine broken."

Now let's explore some consequences other young women have faced as a result of their choices to hook up outside of marriage.

Tiffany: feeling worthless and empty

Tiffany's biological dad left when she was two-and-a-half and her mom remarried about a year after the divorce. In addition, her mom exposed Tiffany to drug use at an early age. Her step-dad Tom went out drinking every night, coming home in the wee hours of the morning. Even though she was a virgin, he yelled at her in drunken rages, calling her a whore, a slut, or a bitch. In the back of her young mind, Tiffany wondered if there was truth to the statements he made.

She lived in a life of extremes. Either Tom would be yelling at her, calling her the worst names one could think of, or he would buy her lavish gifts to make up for his behavior—the newest toy, a bike, expensive skiing trips, and, as she got older, even a new car. When Tiffany asked her mom about his behavior, her mom made excuses for him, saying he was a good man, but he just had some bad habits. Her mom's philosophy in life was to endure through the rough patches and that there was something better coming just around the corner. Though the life

Tiffany had was normal to her, something deep within herself always hoped for something more. She was just surviving a day at a time.

Later, moving into a new community was difficult. Like most fifteen-year-old young women, she wanted a boyfriend and found herself obsessing about her appearance. She chose her outfits each morning with guys in mind, hoping they would glance her way. She read *Teen* magazine, enthralled with articles promising to teach readers "how to get guys to like you." At school, Tiffany followed the girls who were boisterous, outgoing and well-liked. She wanted to be liked, so she naturally migrated towards them.

One night an opportunity came up to go to another party with her new friends. She lied to her parents about where she would be and snuck out to her friends' house to join them at the party. The house was vibrating with loud music. Tiffany recognized a few people from her school, but most of them she didn't know. The guys were ruggedly tall, real men with muscles that tested the limits that their cotton t-shirts would stretch. *There was no way those guys could still be in high school,* she thought. She felt dizzy for a moment as she entered, but kept walking. Taking a beer her friend offered, she followed the lead of her friends, moving from kitchen to couch, smiling timidly when they introduced her to new guys, laughing at the right times in the conversations. She got drunk and started making out with a cute guy who paid attention to her.

Tiffany found herself doing what she didn't want to do—becoming a party girl she knew she wasn't and finding herself in vulnerable places. Sex became an easy way to fit in and feel accepted. Her new lifestyle perpetuated the unhealthy view she had of herself. She was not living a healthy, balanced life with real friends, enjoying healthy relationships, and owning a positive view of herself.

Treating herself like others treated her left her feeling worthless and empty. Because of self-hatred, she started skipping meals, and began struggling with an eating disorder. She hated herself and believed the lies that her stepfather had told her. It was a cycle she was powerless to control. She would battle anorexia for the next nineteen years. What started as simply a desire to be wanted turned into a life she never thought she would have, including having two abortions along the way.

Anna: locking emotions inside

Other girls would talk about how they were saving themselves for the perfect guy or saving themselves for marriage. After being sexually abused, Anna lived with the haunting thought that she had already lost her innocence. Saving herself for anyone didn't really matter to her. She once stated, "I could never give someone that special gift; I could never get it back. I started to do things to please guys, things that I never planned on doing, but I did them anyway. If they were happy, I would be happy. If they could get pleasure out of it, then at least I was worth that much."

Anna bottled up her emotions and kept them locked inside. To cope with the pain, she began cutting her arms and blaming herself for what had happened to her. "I was filled with shame, and I felt as if being raped was something bad that I did. Even the word 'rape' triggered fear in my heart when my friends and people around me would talk about it."

Anna hid behind other coping mechanisms. Achieving academic success, doing well at sports, and pleasing others helped get positive attention from others. These masks were easy to hide behind. "The family discussion of my rape stopped when they thought I was doing well in school and sports," she said. But the trauma sank deep behind the mask.

When we put the mask on and push the trauma down, the survival brain (limbic system) instinctively looks for ways to make us feel better. **Many times the cravings for safety and love cause us to medicate with compulsive behavior**. The trauma Anna and Tiffany faced was not their fault. However, the lies behind the trauma, such as, "I can only be accepted if I am sexual," or "I can't say no or he'll leave," and "there must be something wrong with me that I was raped" lead to medicating the pain with sex, cutting, eating disorders and other compulsive behavior. Often, past trauma can cause women to act in ways they never intended.

  Review the cravings and compulsive behaviors of Tiffany and Anna. With which ones can you relate?

_____

_____

_____

_____

The problem with using sex as a coping mechanism is that it is one of the most dangerous pursuits a young woman can be involved in. Part of walking in authenticity is being willing to look honestly at reality.

Jesus tells the story of a wealthy man who had two sons. The youngest demanded his share of the estate. He then went to a distant land and squandered his fortune on loose living. This Jewish boy ends up in a pigpen feeding swine. (Luke 15)

Have you found yourself in the pigpen of hurtful choices you have made? Let's have a reality check.

Sexual Addiction Screening Test

This test contains questions about your sexual behavior. For this analysis, the terms "sex" and "sexual behavior" refer to any sexual activity including compulsive masturbation, pornography, and/or partnered sexual activity.

Please remember that this test was developed for use with women and men of all ages, with a range of sexual behaviors and experiences.

  Stop now and take the Sexual Addiction Screening Test (SAST-R) that follows.

SEXUAL ADDICTION SCREENING TEST (SAST-R v 2.0)[10]

© 2008, P. J. Carnes, Sexual Addiction Screening Test - Revised
The Sexual Addiction Screening Test (SAST) is designed to assist in the assessment of sexually compulsive or "addictive" behavior. Developed in cooperation with hospitals, treatment programs, private therapists and community groups, the SAST provides a profile of responses that help to discriminate between addictive and non-addictive behavior. To complete the test, answer each question by circling the appropriate yes/no column.

YES	NO	1.	Were you sexually abused as a child or adolescent?
YES	NO	2.	Did your parents have trouble with sexual behavior?
YES	NO	3.	Do you often find yourself preoccupied with sexual thoughts?
YES	NO	4.	Do you feel that your sexual behavior is not normal?
YES	NO	5.	Do you ever feel bad about your sexual behavior?
YES	NO	6.	Has your sexual behavior ever created problems for you and your family?
YES	NO	7.	Have you ever sought help for sexual behavior you did not like?
YES	NO	8.	Has anyone been hurt emotionally because of your sexual behavior?
YES	NO	9.	Are any of your sexual activities against the law?
YES	NO	10.	Have you made efforts to quit a type of sexual activity and failed?
YES	NO	11.	Do you hide some of your sexual behaviors from others?
YES	NO	12.	Have you attempted to stop some parts of your sexual activity?
YES	NO	13.	Have you felt degraded by your sexual behaviors?
YES	NO	14.	When you have sex, do you feel depressed afterwards?
YES	NO	15.	Do you feel controlled by your sexual desire?
YES	NO	16.	Have important parts of your life (such as job, family, friends, leisure activities) been neglected because you were spending too much time on sex?
YES	NO	17.	Do you ever think your sexual desire is stronger than you are?
YES	NO	18.	Is sex almost all you think about?
YES	NO	19.	Has sex (or romantic fantasies) been a way for you to escape your problems?
YES	NO	20.	Has sex become the most important thing in your life?
YES	NO	21.	Are you in crisis over sexual matters?
YES	NO	22.	The internet has created sexual problems for me.
YES	NO	23.	I spend too much time online for sexual purposes.
YES	NO	24.	I have purchased services online for erotic purposes (sites for dating, pornography, fantasy and friend finder).

YES	NO	25.	I have used the internet to make romantic or erotic connections with people online.
YES	NO	26.	People in my life have been upset about my sexual activities online.
YES	NO	27.	I have attempted to stop my online sexual behaviors.
YES	NO	28.	I have subscribed to or regularly purchased or rented sexually explicit materials (magazines, videos, books or online pornography).
YES	NO	29.	I have been sexual with minors.
YES	NO	30.	I have spent considerable time and money on strip clubs, adult bookstores and movie houses.
YES	NO	31.	I have engaged prostitutes and escorts to satisfy my sexual needs.
YE5	NO	32.	I have spent considerable time surfing pornography online.
YES	NO	33.	I have used magazines, videos or online pornography even when there was considerable risk of being caught by family members who would be upset by my behavior.
YES	NO	34.	I have regularly purchased romantic novels or sexually explicit magazines.
YES	NO	35.	I have stayed in romantic relationships after they became emotionally abusive.
YES	NO	36.	I have traded sex for money or gifts.
YES	NO	37.	I have maintained multiple romantic or sexual relationships at the same time.
YES	NO	38.	After sexually acting out, I sometimes refrain from all sex for a significant period.
YES	NO	39.	I have regularly engaged in sadomasochistic behavior.
YES	NO	40.	I visit sexual bath-houses, sex clubs or video/bookstores as part of my regular sexual activity.
YES	NO	41.	I have engaged in unsafe or "risky" sex even though I knew it could cause me harm.
YES	NO	42.	I have cruised public restrooms, rest areas or parks looking for sex with strangers.
YES	NO	43.	I believe casual or anonymous sex has kept me from having more long-term intimate relationships.
YES	NO	44.	My sexual behavior has put me at risk for arrest for lewd conduct or public indecency.
YES	NO	45.	I have been paid for sex.

SAST (Sexual Addiction Screening Test)
Scoring

Scales	Item #	Cut-off (number of "yes" responses). More than the cut-off number indicates a concern in this area	How many "yes" responses did I have?
Core Item scale	1 - 20	6 or more	
Subscales			
Internet items	22 - 27	3 or more	
Men's items	28-33	2 or more	
Women's items	34-39	2 or more	
Homosexual Men	40-45	3 or more	
Addictive Dimensions			
Preoccupation	3, 18, 19, 20	2 or more	
Loss of Control	10,12, 15, 17	2 or more	
Relationship disturbance	6, 8, 16, 26	2 or more	
Affect Disturbance	4, 5, 11, 13, 14	2 or more	

Relative Distributions of Addict & Non-Addict SAST Scores

This instrument has been based on screenings of tens of thousands of people. This particular version is a developmental stage revision of the instrument, so scoring may be adjusted with more research. Please be aware that clinical decisions must be made conditionally since final scoring protocols may vary.

Putting the SAST-R Results in Perspective

Your SAST scores help give you an objective way of discerning where you are in your journey of healing. The test isn't designed to condemn you, so don't view it as something to pass or fail. Instead, the SAST helps you see the depth of your problem. For example, replying "yes" to six or more of the first twenty questions indicates that the process of healing may take awhile. You are facing a spiritual and emotional battle that cannot be won alone. You must be willing to be supported by those in your Behind the Mask group.

Even if you scored below six in the first twenty questions, you may still have areas where you struggle with powerlessness. You can't seem to stop certain sexual behaviors. Here are some examples from other young women:

- Whenever I am alone and bored, I feel compelled to be sexual.
- I masturbate myself to sleep at times and I hate it.
- I can't stop making out with my boyfriend—and we do a lot more than just kiss each other.
- At times I can't stay off Internet porn sites on my computer or cell phone.
- Sometimes I sext pictures and suggestive messages to boys.
- I roam the TV channels at times looking for suggestive programs.

  How many "yes" responses do you have to questions 1 to 20? _____

  If you scored "yes" to 6 or more of the questions from 1 to 20, you, like the prodigal, have journeyed to a distant land of dangerous pursuits. Whether you scored more than six or less than six, summarize your journey into the pigpen using the space below. Draw, use words, or in some other way create a picture of your journey.

Few stories that Jesus told have become more popular and have touched the human heart so deeply. The language is vivid, emotions raw, and the pictures are unforgettable. Read Luke 15:17-24 to see what happens when the prodigal son comes home.

"When he finally came to his senses, he said to himself, 'At home even the hired servants have food enough to spare, and here I am dying of hunger! I will go home to my father and say, "Father, I have sinned against both heaven and you, and I am no longer worthy of being called your son. Please take me on as a hired servant."'

"So he returned home to his father. And while he was still a long way off, his father saw him coming. Filled with love and compassion, he ran to his son, embraced him, and kissed him. His son said to him, 'Father, I have sinned against both heaven and you, and I am no longer worthy of being called your son.'

"But his father said to the servants, 'Quick! Bring the finest robe in the house and put it on him. Get a ring for his finger and sandals for his feet. And kill the calf we have been fattening. We must celebrate with a feast, for this son of mine was dead and has now returned to life. He was lost, but now he is found.' So the party began."

Luke 15:17-24 (NLT)

☙ As you read the story, how did you relate it to your life?

_____

_____

_____

_____

_____

The prodigal headed home only after he had run out of his own resources and realized he was powerless to provide even his basic needs. The same is true for us until we realize that we have been on a highway of destruction and are powerless to change direction on our own. The reason we can be so blind to the highway we are travelling is that there is something in that "high-way" that has a deep emotional appeal to us: The high of masturbating, the buzz of another conquest or romantic relationship, or the thrill of doing something that you know is wrong or dangerous. It is all about medicating the pain deep within. We are so fixated on avoiding the deep pain that we don't even know we are on the highway.

At some point you have to push the "pause" button and ask the question, "Is this the path I really want to be on in life?" The path you are on will determine where you ultimately end up. Is this where you really want to go? Those are hard questions to ask because you can get caught up in the here and now, much like the prodigal who was focused on his own pleasure and needs.[11]

So how do you get off the highway that leads to the pigpen? First, recognize the dangerous road you have been traveling.

☙ List some possible negative consequences that you think can result from sexual activity before marriage.

_____

_____

_____

PHYSICAL DANGERS

The Prodigal enjoyed the distant land for a season and then the pigpen reality struck. The first pigpen reality of sexual pursuits you may have faced is the physical dangers that include **STD's** (sexually transmitted diseases) and/or **pregnancy**.

There are three types of STD's: Viral, Parasitic and Bacterial. Perhaps you know someone who is suffering from one of the following infections:

1. Viral STD's do not have a cure and they include the following:

- **HIV/AIDS** attacks the immune system. Approximately 1.2 million people in the United States are living with HIV infection, according to November 2011 statistics from the United States CDC (Centers for Disease Control).[12]

- **HPV,** the most common STD, includes over 40 types that can infect the genitals, mouth and throat. Some of these strains cause genital warts and others can cause cancer of the cervix, vulva, vagina, penis, anus, tongue, tonsils, and throat. The immune system will clear 90% of the cases of HPV within 2 years. HPV is so common at least 50% of sexually active men and women will get it at some point in their life.[13]

- **Genital Herpes** is a chronic viral infection that lasts a lifetime. Most cases are transmitted by those who are unaware they have the infection or are not experiencing symptoms. About one of every six people in the United States have genital herpes. Symptoms include blisters, itching sores, and fever that can emerge two weeks after being infected and can last two to four weeks, with periodic outbreaks that last a lifetime.[14]

- **Hepatitis B/C,** a blood disease that can be sexually transmitted, affects the liver and can causes life-long infections, scarring of the liver, liver cancer, liver failure, and death.[15]

☙ **After reading these facts about Viral STD's, summarize in your own words the dangers of sexual activity outside of marriage.**

_____

_____

_____

_____

_____

_____

2. Parasitic STD's are treatable by a doctor:

Trichomoniasis is the most common curable STD in sexually active young women. This parasite is sexually transmitted through intercourse or genital contact with an infected partner. Most men have no signs or symptoms while some women do. Symptoms include a frothy, yellow-green vaginal discharge with a strong odor.[16]

3. Bacterial STD's are treatable by a doctor:

- **Chlamydia** is the most frequently reported STD in the U.S. Sometimes there are no symptoms; it can cause Pelvic Inflammatory Disease (PID) and infertility.[17]

- **Gonorrhea** can cause pelvic pain in women and a puss discharge from the penis in men. Sometimes there are no symptoms in either gender. It can cause infertility.[18]

- **Syphilis** progresses through three stages if not treated. The third stage can occur ten to twenty years after the first infection and can severely damage internal organs including the brain. It can also cause dementia and death.[19]

Nearly all STDs can be transmitted through vaginal, oral and anal sex. There are 19 million new STD cases occurring each year in the U.S. and almost half of these are in people ages 14 to 24.[20]

Unplanned Pregnancy. The second physical outcome of dangerous sexual pursuits outside of marriage is an unplanned pregnancy. Essentially there are four choices you can make, none of which are easy, and all are life changing.

4 choices
- Become a single mom, which can alter or adjust your dreams and goals.
- Put the child up for adoption, which is a heart wrenching, yet a courageous and loving decision, considering there are so many couples waiting to adopt.
- Abortion, which is removal of the baby from the mother's womb, not only ends a life but also causes the mom future agony regarding her decision, especially when viewed in light of her Christian commitment.
- The safe haven law in some states allows an infant up to 72 hours old to be left with a qualified person at one of two locations—the emergency room at a hospital or a fire station during its hours of operation. The birth mother will avoid any criminal prosecution for this action in states that have adopted this law.

✑ **Summarize what you would share about the physical dangers of sex before marriage with a young woman considering becoming sexually active.**

_____

_____

_____

_____

LEGAL DANGERS

If you send or receive sexual images you can be legally charged with creating or distributing child pornography. If you keep any sexual images of your peers, you could be charged with possession of child porn even if you were not the picture-taker.[21]

EMOTIONAL DANGERS

As mentioned, we can find ourselves on the highway of dangerous pursuits because of the emotional high it engenders. The dopamine high can cause us, like the prodigal, to make regrettable choices. Many young women report the emotional distress of having been dumped by a boyfriend after being sexual with him. They describe feelings of being used, loss of reputation, depression, regret, anger, hurt, and fear. These emotions can affect the level of trust in future relationships. Trauma can have long lasting effects.

❧ **If you have experienced being dumped in a relationship, what were you feeling emotionally and spiritually?**

_____

_____

SPIRITUAL DANGERS

Sexual intercourse was created by God to connect and bond us with the opposite sex in a marriage relationship. God intended that our sexual relationship would literally glue people together as husband and wife. Genesis 2:24 (KJV) says that we *"become one flesh."* This can be illustrated with paper and glue; when two pieces of paper are glued together and then pulled apart, pieces of each paper are stuck to the other. The same is true when premarital sex takes place. Physical, spiritual, and emotional attachments between lovers remain even when the relationship ends. The enemy will use these attachments against the individuals. Listen to what Jordi says at age 33:

> *"The hardest breakup I ever had was with the first person I had sex with. Fifteen years later, I still don't think I am over him. I still dream about him and think about him and compare every guy since then to him. I'm married now and I feel like it's a threesome in my heart. It is like he is still a part of me and I still can't get over him."*[22]

If you, like the prodigal, have found yourself in a distant land, part of turning around will be to admit you have been powerless to stop your past choices. You may have thought, "I can change directions all by myself. I don't need help." The truth is that you will remain in the pigpen until you face the places you have been powerless.

Points and places of feeling powerless over unwanted behaviors

Here are some examples of what others have said in the past:

- I end up going all the way when I promised myself I wouldn't.
- I am sexually inappropriate when it comes to Internet/chat-room activity.
- I masturbate to get rid of the stress.
- I fantasize and masturbate to avoid problems.
- I go to parties and drink too much and . . . . .
- I can't refuse guys that come on to me.
- I can't control myself when I hear certain music.
- When I sit down at the computer I don't intend to go to _____ sites, but I always seem to end up at those places.
- I have hooked up with guys to feel wanted and loved.

❧ **List your unwanted behaviors, how you have tried to stop each behavior, and what you feel when you lose the battle.**

Unwanted behavior	Ways I have tried to stop the behavior	What I feel when I lose the battle

Like the prodigal who rehearsed the fact that he had sinned against his father and heaven, you will need to be honest about the unwanted behaviors with which you have struggled. You will continue to find yourself in the distant land if those struggle points remain hidden. Secrets in themselves are a problem because it becomes difficult to remember what lies you told to whom so you aren't discovered. Add to that the constant fear of being discovered and the guilt and shame of knowing you are being dishonest. You are as sick as your secrets because soon you believe the stories you have told others. Reality becomes distorted and you begin to live the lie behind a mask. Courage can only be based on reality and a decision to take off the mask. This is the only path that will lead to a journey of authenticity.

❧ **Write a prayer asking God to help you share with your group the unwanted behaviors that leave you feeling powerless, and how you feel when you lose the battle. God, like the prodigal father and your *Behind the Mask* group, will continue to love you and be accepting of your desire to come out from the distant land into a new place of freedom.**

_____

_____

_____

_____

_____

_____

_____

_____

One of the reasons you will be writing and then telling your story in the weeks to come is the same reason Jesus told so many stories. Recent discoveries in neuroscience reveal the genius of His approach. Research has uncovered the fact that narratives require the participation of multiple structures throughout the brain. They require us to bring together our knowledge, sensations, feelings, and behaviors. In this process, multiple functions from different neural networks are brought together, providing the brain with the tools for both emotional and neural integration.[23]

Implication: Telling your story **truthfully** in a safe environment heals you! That is because your brain is profoundly changed when you tell your story. When Amnesty International began helping torture victims they had little, if any, positive results. The victims resisted help at every level despite the fact they were miserable. Then the organization discovered that if the torture victims could tell their painful story in a room full of individuals who were also torture victims, they would finally receive healing. [24]

If you scored six or more on the SAST-R, more than likely you have experienced trauma at some point in your life. I have learned a healing truth through the years. If you know the woman's trauma story then you know her addiction story. The next chapter will include a place for you to write out your story.

Once the secrets are finally pulled out of the closet, you can start telling your story of how things can be. Usually telling your story will include revealing how bad things are and how desperate you are. It is a starting point. But eventually your story will include God's answer to your desperation. Storytelling under the grace of God is about change.[25]

& **How are you feeling about telling your story to the group? Please share honestly!**

What are your fears?

_____

_____

_____

What are your hopes?

_____

_____

_____

Finally, as you think about writing your story, consider the unlikely women who show up in the genealogy of Christ. Only five women are mentioned in Matthew's account of the genealogy and all had been soiled by a fallen world.

Matthew 1:3   Tamar posed as a prostitute, and tricked Judah into having sex with her. (Genesis 38)
Matthew 1:5   Rahab was a prostitute. (Joshua 2:1)
Matthew 1:5   Ruth the Moabitess was a Gentile. (Ruth 1)
Matthew 1:6   Bathsheba, referred to as the wife of Uriah, with whom David had sex and then had her husband killed. (2 Samuel 11-12)
Matthew 1:16   Mary the mother of Jesus, whose reputation was questioned.

Matthew is communicating loud and clear that God has constantly moved in unusual ways to achieve His purposes, even within the kingly lineage of Christ. God is not averse to using those who lack respectability. In fact, He is constantly reaching out to empower the most unlikely to be His supernatural agents. Their past did not disqualify them from the purposes of God and neither does yours.[26]

Song recommendation for meditation this week:
Easier Than Love
By Switchfoot

Mask of the Day

Chapter 4
The Mind Behind the Mask

Cindy   *"One thing the church never tells you before you have sex is how good it will feel. I mean, your body will respond to the touch of a man. We are made that way! My issue came when I mistook that feeling as evidence that what I was doing with my boyfriend outside of marriage was good for me."*

Most of us will do things that make us feel better at the moment, even if we understand those things could hurt us in the future. A simple example is how we eat. Many people choose to make frequent trips to fast food restaurants knowing that such choices can lead to heart disease or death in the distant future. Only those who discipline their brains will have the mental strength to avoid too many french fries or that second piece of chocolate cake. Those who think about the future and make disciplined choices usually live longer and have healthier lives.

After counseling women for three decades I (Diane) have come to see that the most significant difference between immaturity and maturity is the ability to delay gratification for a higher cause. A young woman with maturity will choose to wait, delaying immediate gratification for a higher cause. Immaturity in a young woman says, "I want to have what I want now!"[27]

There are many obstacles in waiting. Before the twentieth century there was no such thing as a "teenager." Young men and women got married by the age of 14 or 15.[28] Hormone changes and brain changes in a young adolescent add to the difficulty of waiting. Most young adults are waiting until their early or middle twenties to get married. The widening gap between when one's body is able to produce offspring and the age men and women are choosing to marry poses a challenge for those wanting to walk in sexual purity before marriage.

≥ **What struggles have you had in "waiting"?**

_____

_____

_____

_____

Sexual Progression
Studies show that the key to waiting and abstaining is directly correlated to limiting the amount of time spent together alone and the amount of sexual arousal that takes place.

Take Cindy, for example. The moment that she saw Luke, her eyes soaked in visual information about his looks—his eye color, his stature, his face symmetry, his height, his smile. Her brain processed this information within a network of neurons, and her mind concluded he was a viable, healthy partner with whom she could mate and produce healthy babies. In her words, he was "hot." When Cindy got close enough, she breathed in his scent. Chemicals from Luke's skin, called pheromones, entered her nostrils. Pheromone receptors in her cells connected with Luke's scent, and now they had "chemistry." He spoke to her in complimentary sentences, and her brain went into overdrive trying to decode the meaning behind the words. Flashes of a future with him—a wedding, two kids, and a big house—grew in her imagination. Her prefrontal cortex reminded her that she is too young to get married, that she doesn't have a job, nor does he. However, that part of her brain will not fully form until she turns 25. Thus, logic loses.

Since she entered puberty in middle school, her levels of estrogen have been surging, causing bonding chemicals of dopamine and oxytocin to flood the brain. Cindy feels better than she has ever felt, connected to Luke more every time they spend time together. She feels "high" in a floaty kind of way, and she hasn't even kissed Luke yet! At night when she lays down, she wonders if she is in love.

By the time Luke invites Cindy into the basement to cuddle on the couch, the struggle in her mind between her logical brain and her survival/sexual brain has escalated. The more she tries to resist, the more anxious she becomes and a need for relief from the conflict develops. Add a deep wound from her father and a life-long inner need to be held, and you have a recipe for compromise.

As Luke touches Cindy's arm and kisses her face, the fire that has been burning inside her turns to fireworks. The hormones are raging, but there are also chemicals that are being released in the brain—endorphins and enkephalins—that produce feelings of pleasure and satisfaction. As Cindy's body and brain react to his touch, she is aroused, and her body is ready to accept a man. Cindy still has a choice: she can follow her physical instincts and choose to go the whole way, or she can leave the situation. "Slowing down" is almost impossible. How Cindy has trained her brain will determine how she responds to this situation.

The reasonable definition of sexual activity suggested by recent brain studies indicates that sexual activity is any intimate contact between two individuals that involves arousal, stimulation, and/or a response by at least one of the two partners. In other words, **sexual activity is intentional sexually intimate behavior between two partners, or even one person if self-stimulation is used**. Sexual excitement starts in the brain.[29] Thus, a definition of sexual activity must not only include sexual intercourse but also anal sex, oral sex, mutual masturbation, showering together, fondling of breasts—all of these produce sexual stimulation and gratification.

Are you a runner or an athlete? Are you a musician, writer, or artist? Do you love to have deep conversations with someone close to you? Any of these activities will get these pleasurable brain chemicals going, but if any of these activities becomes the primary focus of the brain, life can get out of balance; that is especially true with the sexual pathway. When our bodies are aroused we can condition or train our brains to respond in a certain way.

The Brain
Let's look at the brain for a minute. If you put your two fists together, this emulates the size of your brain. It only weighs three pounds and makes up only 2% of your body mass, yet it uses 25% of the oxygen and 20% of the calories you consume daily. Your brain is composed of 80% water and has the consistency of butter at room temperature.

Your brain is the most complex of God's creations. It has **100 billion neurons** and each of those have upwards of **10,000 connections**. This means that there are more neurological connections in your brain than there are stars in the entire universe.

These neurons do not come pre-wired, but are "wired" according to the experiences a person has after birth. Inside the brain is the Amygdala, or the survival brain, which is fully formed by age six.

The pre-frontal cortex, which is not fully developed until your mid-twenties, allows you to make good decisions; it is your higher reasoning center and also helps you to stop dangerous behavior.

When a girl reaches adolescence, **her brain is literally sprouting, reorganizing and pruning neurological circuits that drive the way she thinks, feels, and acts**. She spends long hours looking into the mirror and judging herself against her peers, media images, and other attractive females.

Amygdala

Why do girls all decide to go to the bathroom together? Scientists have found that in the teen years the flood of estrogen in the girl's brain will activate oxytocin, which is a bonding chemical, and dopamine. Dopamine is the chemical that makes you feel high on boys, obsess about them and can't get them out of your mind. These two chemicals are released in the female brain especially when girls are hanging out, flirting, or talking about boys. A girl engaged in these activities is getting high on her own drugs her brain is making! What has all this got to do with sexuality? When married, these two chemicals help us bond with, and become one with, our mate.

It is a trap to believe that the guy you are now dating is "the one." That doesn't mean the relationship isn't valuable or significant, but it does mean you are dealing with a dopamine high. Dr. Helen Fisher did a fascinating study about what happens to the brain when you fall in love. When your brain is activated by romance, the dopamine levels go through the roof.[30] Another way of putting this is that you feel so high you start acting like a dope. Dr. Fisher commented in one lecture, "When you are in love you shouldn't be allowed to drive because you are on drugs." These drugs are the ones your brain is releasing into your system. You can't think about anything but him. He is your obsession! Fortunately, this temporary insanity soon passes as your brain prepares to transition to the long-term commitment of marriage.[31]

Now, maybe you can understand the mental pressures you feel in the dating process. You experience high levels of estrogen-progesterone monthly surges as you ovulate and menstruate; with these surges emotions can become reactive to relational stress. For young women, the main stress is the need to be liked and socially connected. Again, oxytocin is a chemical in the brain that gives you that sense of closeness and intimacy.[32] Estrogen at puberty increases dopamine and oxytocin. When these chemicals are released, they hit the pleasure center of the brain that gives you the biggest neurological reward you can get outside of an orgasm.[33]

When your dopamine level peaks, then you fall in love with this guy. It's neurological fireworks! The huge problem is, this probably isn't the guy you will eventually marry. You are in what I call an "Exile Time" spiritually. You are in a place you don't want to be. God has called you to sexual purity when your emotional desires are at full speed.[34]

The Bible is filled with people struggling with exile moments. One is when Jeremiah challenges his people, who are caught up in exile, to trust God.

> *This is what the LORD says: "You will be in Babylon for seventy years. But then I will come and do for you all the good things I have promised, and I will bring you home again. For I know the plans I have for you," says the LORD. "They are plans for good and not for disaster, to give you a future and a hope. In those days when you pray, I will listen. If you look for me wholeheartedly, you will find me."*
> Jeremiah 29:10-13 (NLT)

Jeremiah essentially told Israel not to listen to the false dreams of the phony prophets because those false dreams interfere with *honest living*. They are in exile in Babylon and they are going to face a long time of being in a place they didn't want to be. Just like your challenge of being in a time of intense sexual temptation when God calls you to walk in purity. The truth is, you will probably be in a **sexual Babylon** for a decade. But the only place you have to trust God is where you are right now.

The false prophets of our day and age are declaring, "Go ahead, premarital sex is normal. Everyone is doing it." You are in a battle; the enemy will try to cut to the core of your belief system because you are no greater than what you believe under pressure. That is why you are not going to defeat the enemy by willpower. Just trying harder not to masturbate, hook-up, or cross "the line" sexually—WILL NOT WORK. You need the POWER OF GOD to transform your mind.

❧ **What has "trying harder" looked like in your life?**

_____

_____

_____

_____

_____

_____

The challenge is to believe God when your hormones are driving you over the cliff; to believe God when you can't see His hand at work and you are tempted to go places that violate your value system; to believe God when the harder you try not to do something, the worse it seems to get. I love what Jesus said to Peter: **"Simon, Simon, Satan has asked to sift you as wheat. But I have prayed for you, Simon, that your faith may not fail. And when you have turned back, strengthen your brothers."** (Luke 22:31-32 NIV)

The more Peter tried to do things on his own the worse it got and he couldn't even understand why it wasn't working. You may be in the same situation trying to follow Christ with all your heart but failing sexually time after time. In fact, you might have promised yourself each time that you will never do it again. I am sure that Peter made those same kinds of promises. He was in an exile of the deepest kind. But the thing that kept him going was this fact: Jesus prayed for him. He prayed for him, all the while knowing his weaknesses and struggles, his traumas and trials, and also his deepest fears and insecurities. Christ prayed that Peter wouldn't lose his faith.

I have seen young women lose their passion for Christ because of their romantic and sexual struggles. They never realized that Christ was praying for them the whole time. They gave up the battle, missing the truth that Christ would never give up on them.

> **In what areas have you been tempted to give up on yourself?**

_____

_____

_____

The King James Bible translation of Luke 22:31-32 uses interesting terminology for the phrase "when you have turned back." It says, "When you are converted." Peter is not some belligerent sinner. He has literally given up everything to follow Christ. Jesus is talking about Peter finally becoming the man God had in mind when He originally created him. Jesus was saying to Peter, "There is something down inside of you I am going to bring out of you in this time of exile that will result in you becoming a whole other guy!"

When you come to Christ, a *finished work of grace* takes place that converts your spirit, but it signals the beginning of a *progressive work of grace* to convert your soul. Scripture defines your soul as your will, intellect, and emotions. And the hardware of your soul is your brain. When you don't understand this truth you can read promises in the Bible like . . .

- *I can do all things in Christ.*
- *I am more than a conqueror in Christ.*
- *Old things have passed away and behold all things have become new.*

. . . and become profoundly frustrated because they just don't seem to be true in your sexual life. Instead, remember that your soul needs to be renewed. Your mind needs to be renewed if you are going to fully experience these promises. You have to literally reprogram your mind. Science has finally caught up with biblical truth, now showing evidence that you can actually, physically renew your mind. The amazing ability your mind has to adapt and modify to your environment is called neuroplasticity.[35]

Many people think of their brain as some sort of container and learning as simply putting something in it. When they try to break a bad habit they think it's simply a matter of putting something new into it—like a Bible verse, a prayer, or trying really hard. But when we learn a bad habit, that "brain space" is not available for good habits.

Recent research reveals the best policy is to learn the good habit early on, before the bad habit gets a neurological competitive advantage. Hell understands this fact; that's why most young men start struggling with masturbation and porn in their early teen years. Often young women also struggle with this when they hit puberty. Your spiritual adversary will attack as soon as he can because he wants to claim some ground in your brain when you are still young.

Cindy's advice: *"If you had a wild phase, or if you slept with someone last night and regret it in the morning, are you going to stay in the dumps? Or are you going to forgive yourself and take the high road, learning from your mistakes? The more you tell yourself that you are a slut, that you are worthless, the more Satan wants to keep you there. He will continually remind you of your mistakes because he doesn't want you to have freedom or to experience the grace that God has for you.*

God takes those situations and makes beauty from ashes. He will take the mess you made for yourself and use it as an opportunity to build your character and bring you closer to Him."

❧ **Draw a picture showing how the enemy's schemes in the past have tried to dominate your life.** Show what weapons the enemy has used against you. Examples might include lies, hurts from the past, loneliness, stress, etc.

Once sexual bondage takes root in your soul, it changes the literal structure of your brain. It stops being just a moral problem; it has now become a brain problem. That's precisely why you can't stop your behavior no matter how many times you promise yourself you will. The key is renewing your mind by clearing out the old mental files.

Jesus says to you the same thing he declared to Peter, "When you are converted." Not if or maybe you will be converted but **when.** Therefore, if you hang on to Jesus as you walk through this book, being diligent to do all the assignments, I promise you that you will re-set your brain and see victory in your behavior. When you courageously make a decision to face your issues with the help of other young women in your group, Jesus will pull you through. But you have to be looking in the right direction. Jesus told Peter, "When you are converted you will strengthen your brothers." **You have to look beyond yourself!**

In counseling young women over the years, I know they are going to successfully make it if one thing takes place: if they start grasping the fact they need to face the pain in their life and that God will eventually use their pain to help others. You will ignite a revolution sparked by young women like you who decide to walk in freedom and then turn and help others come to purity. This is the key battle for your generation. Hell thinks it has your generation by the throat spiritually because of sexual bondage. But victory can rise up from you and your friends that will devastate the devil's plans!

How does victory take place?[36]

Because your brain has literally been hijacked in battle, you need some incredibly powerful weapons to set you free. You must commit yourself completely to: 1) Hard work and honesty and 2) Taking up the Sword of the Spirit.

Commitment #1: Hard Work and Honesty

Different than trying harder to stop a behavior, this discipline includes working hard at facing your reality and destroying denial. Hard work and honesty are foreign territory for those dealing with compulsive sexual issues. You may be a hard worker and deeply honest in many areas of your life, but with respect to your sexuality this may not be true. The hard work with respect to you getting free is especially going to be difficult because you can't be in control, which is where the honesty comes in.

Your *Behind the Mask* group will be a place where your honesty will be tested. In answering the questions in this book you can hide if you want to, but I pray that your group becomes a place where nothing is hidden. I pray that it becomes a place where you finally open up. Please choose to trust some other young women totally and be open to their feedback even when it is painful and revealing.

The following pages suggest things you can do, things to accept, and things to which you can commit. Each section contains practical helps for moving toward healthy sexuality.[37]

Things I Can Do:

- **Attend a small group regularly.**
- **God's values supersede mine; therefore, I will contend to live life on His terms instead of my terms or those of the culture around me.**
- **Pay close attention to what I look at, what I listen to, what I set my mind on.**
- **Take responsibility for my thoughts and actions.**
- **Verbally describe my feelings.**
- **Make contact with a group member at least twice between small group meetings.**

A commitment to these things will help you continue to grow in self-awareness and keep you from isolating. Making contacts with group members outside group time is incredibly important.

   How easy or difficult is it for you to commit to each of these six items? (1 = easy; 5= difficult) Circle your response.

Things I Can Do:

1. Attend a small group regularly.   1   2   3   4   5

2. God's values supersede mine; therefore, I will contend to live life on His terms instead of mine or of the culture around me.   1   2   3   4   5

3. Pay close attention to what I look at; what I listen to: what I set my mind on. 1   2   3   4   5

4. Take responsibility for my thoughts and actions.   1   2   3   4   5

5. Verbally describe my feelings.   1   2   3   4   5

6. Make contact with a group member at least twice between small group meetings.

         1   2   3   4   5

In his studies of the original language of the New Testament, Pastor Harry Flanagan discovered that over 80% of the time the word "heal" and its derivative appear in the Bible text, they come from the Greek word "therapeuo" from which we get our word "therapy." Pastor Harry says, *"The intended meaning is a process. Healing requires you to become honest with yourself by acknowledging the lies of commission and omission. It requires breaking isolation and facing the pain in life. The isolation and secrecy that feel so comfortable actually keep you in bondage to your addictive life."*[38]

I Can Accept:

*   **Healing is a miraculous process over time.**
*   **Healing requires feeling the pain and learning from it.**
*   **I am very capable of retreating back into the addictive or unhealthy lifestyle.**
*   **A relapse does not stop the healing process, but will have consequences.**
*   **I have become skilled at lying to others and myself.**
*   **I do not really live in isolation; my choices do affect others.**
*   **My secrecy keeps me in bondage to my sin.**

> **How easy or difficult is it for you to accept each of these seven items?** (1 = easy; 5 = difficult) Circle your response.

I can accept:

1. Healing is a miraculous process over time.   1   2   3   4   5

2. Healing requires feeling the pain and learning from it.   1   2   3   4   5

3. I am very capable of retreating back into the addictive or unhealthy lifestyle. 1   2   3   4   5

4. A relapse does not stop the healing process, but will have consequences. 1   2   3   4   5

5. I have become skilled at lying to others and myself.   1   2   3   4   5

6. I do not really live in isolation; my choices do affect others. 1   2   3   4   5

7. My secrecy keeps me in bondage to my sin.   1   2   3   4   5

I Will Commit To:

*   **A willingness to change—and follow through with my plans.**
*   **Total confidentiality! I discuss only <u>my</u> experiences outside the group.**
*   **Rigorous honesty with God, my small group, myself, and eventually with my friends and family.**
*   **Building my knowledge base (books, CD's, DVD's and seminars).**
*   **Reading Scripture and praying.**
*   **A biblical standard of sexual purity in my life.**
*   **A goal of moving toward sobriety that is living life God's way.**

✎ **How easy or difficult is it for you to commit to each of these items?** (1= easy; 5=difficult) Circle your response.

I Will Commit To:

1. A willingness to change—and follow through with my plans.   1   2   3   4   5

2. Total confidentiality! I discuss only <u>my</u> experiences outside the group. 1   2   3   4   5

3. Rigorous honesty with God, my small group, myself, and eventually with my friends and family.   1   2   3   4   5

4. Building my knowledge base (Books, CD's, DVD's and seminars).   1   2   3   4   5

5. Reading Scripture and praying.   1   2   3   4   5

6. A biblical standard of sexual purity in my life.   1   2   3   4   5

7. A goal of moving toward sobriety that is living life God's way.   1   2   3   4   5

✎ **If you are willing to commit to the healing process, sign the Covenant to Contend as it appears on the one-page version included with this chapter. Ask your group leader or co-leader to sign as a witness.**

> *Healing is a process that requires you to become honest with yourself. It requires breaking isolation and facing the pain in life.*

A Covenant To Contend:

The Courageous Fight For Healthy Sexuality

Things I Can Do:
- Attend a small group regularly.
- God's values supersede mine; therefore, I will contend to live life on His terms instead of my terms or those of the culture around me.
- Pay close attention to what I look at, what I listen to, what I set my mind on.
- Take responsibility for my thoughts and actions.
- Verbally describe my feelings.
- Make contact with a group member at least twice between small group meetings.

I Can Accept:
- Healing is a miraculous process over time.
- Healing requires feeling the pain and learning from it.
- I am very capable of retreating back into the addictive or unhealthy lifestyle.
- A relapse does not stop the healing process, but it will have consequences.
- I have become skilled at lying to others and myself.
- I do not really live in isolation; my choices do affect others.
- My secrecy keeps me in bondage to my sin.

I Will Commit To:
- A willingness to change—and follow through with my plans.
- **Total confidentiality!** I discuss only **my** experiences outside the group.
- Rigorous honesty with God, my small group, myself and eventually to my friends and family.
- Building my knowledge base (books, CD's, videos, & seminars).
- Reading Scripture and praying.
- A biblical standard of sexual purity in my life.
- A goal of moving toward sobriety that is living life God's way.

Signed: _____ Date: _____

Witnessed by: _____

Commitment #2: Take up the Sword of the Spirit in your life!

Paul makes a critical observation in his description of the warrior God has designed you to become:

Take the helmet of salvation and the sword of the Spirit, which is the word of God.
Ephesians 6:17 (NIV)

This is the only offensive weaponry Paul mentions in the complete description of a Roman soldier. Everything else enables the warrior to stand against the enemy's assaults. Therefore, you must have this spiritual weapon in your battle.

What is Paul talking about? Fortunately, he makes it very clear. It is the Word of God that you need, but not just in a general sense. Paul uses the phrase "*The sword of the Spirit which is the rhema of God.*" The sword is given to you by the Holy Spirit.[39] This is why Paul used the term *rhema* (revealed word) instead of *logos* (written word).

God the Holy Spirit will be speaking promises to you as you walk through this journey. When He speaks, **write those thoughts down and review them every morning in your quiet time.** You must have a God-given dream to make it through the battle. You need something with which you can cut into the enemy when you feel like quitting, or when you are experiencing cravings that are driving you crazy. You need something when you are feeling worthless and like a failure, or when your mind is sliding towards the cliff of relapse once again. You need to take a stand with God's promise to you in your hand, His dream in your heart, and the women in your *Behind the Mask* group standing beside you. Then you will realize you have been captured by God's grace for total victory!

Cindy's "rhema word" or "prophetic promise" that the Holy Spirit spoke to her through her healing process is this: *"You are not damaged goods, you are my daughter."* She had seen herself as damaged goods for years, and lived accordingly. Cindy was living a lie until she heard the Holy Spirit say to her heart, *"You are not damaged goods, you are my daughter."* A new truth has replaced the lie. Cindy is the daughter of a King, and is free to live as royalty.

> **Song recommendation for meditation this week:**
> ## *Take Anchor*
> ### *by Christina Mulkey*

ϡ Writing out your story is where you can begin the commitment of doing the hard work and being honest. In the lines provided and using some of what you have discovered about yourself in previous chapters, write a brief story about your relational and/or sexual struggles.

_____

_____

_____

_____

_____

_____

_____

_____

_____

_____

_____

_____

_____

_____

_____

_____

_____

_____

_____

_____

_____

_____

_____

_____

❧ Draw a picture or make a collage of what you want your life to look like when you win this battle. Spend time listening to God and allow Him to prophetically speak as you create this picture or collage.

This is my God-given dream . . .

∾ Spend some time in God's word and find a *rhema* word—a personal promise God is making to you.

_____

_____

_____

_____

_____

_____

"Choices"
One angel wing, one bat wing:
Every day—choices between God & the world

Chapter 5
Uncovering the Real Battle

Jessica

As a sophomore in college, Jessica met a guy with whom she knew she wanted to be more than friends. A month after they started hanging out, she found herself in her first serious boyfriend/girlfriend relationship. Jessica took it slow and waited until he told her he loved her before she kissed him. She kept her walls up, holding onto God's promise for her that sex in marriage would be best. Three years down the road, they married and on their wedding day got wild and crazy with each other. There was an innocent freedom that Jessica got to experience with her husband that few of her friends would ever know. Even later in her marriage when she faced challenging times, Jessica had less sexual bondage to break free from, and could focus her heart on healing without wading through regrets of her past.

Sexual abstinence before marriage has long been perceived as a religious position rather than a scientifically suggested course of action. The wisdom of abstaining prior to marriage can now be validated with brain research studies. "But now, **with the aid of modern neuroscience and a wealth of research, it is evident that humans are the healthiest and happiest when they engage in sex only with the one who is their mate for a lifetime.**" [40]

Here are some discoveries others have made about their sexuality:

"It wasn't easy, but I am so glad we waited. I'm healthy, I love my wife, and I just don't have the baggage some of my friends do." - Rick, age 30. [41]

> *"I thought when I found the right person and married I would be able to leave behind my promiscuous lifestyle as a young adult. But since I married, I have had numerous encounters with men. When men look at me, I melt. It is like waking a sleeping giant that I have no control over. I have tried praying and asking God to help me. 1 Corinthians 10:13 says, 'No temptation has seized you, except what is common to man. And God is faithful…. He will provide a way out.' I admitted to God I have a problem but where is my way out? Is He really there for me?"* - Kim

Kim's testimony challenges us to ask a lot of questions. Where is God when I really need Him? Isn't He there to help me in time of need? If God's word is true, where is the freedom?

Let's begin answering these questions with another question. What is your picture of God?

✎ In the box below, draw a picture of God in relationship to your life. Where is He? Where are you?

If you were to ask Kim to do this exercise, I imagine her drawing a picture of herself in the far bottom left hand corner and a big eye in the sky in the top right hand corner. Sometimes it is hard to see and feel God even when we have said "yes" to Jesus and asked Him into our lives.

Why is that? One reason is our view of God. Many see Him as an up-tight parent or a traffic cop waiting for us to mess up or as an airport security screener rifling through our moral suitcases looking for our vices. Jesus tried to shatter that picture by sharing the parable of the lost son who went to a distant land. We looked at the son's departure in a previous chapter; now let's look at his return from the pigpen as he comes to his senses.

> *I'm going back to my father. I'll say to him, 'Father, I've sinned against God, I've sinned before you; I don't deserve to be called your son. Take me on as a hired hand.' He got right up and went home to his father. When he was still a long way off, his father saw him. His heart pounding, he ran out, embraced him, and kissed him. The son started his speech: 'Father, I've sinned against God, I've sinned before you; I don't deserve to be called your son ever again.'*
>
> *But the father wasn't listening. He was calling to the servants, 'Quick. Bring a clean set of clothes and dress him. Put the family ring on his finger and sandals on his feet. Then get a grain-fed heifer and roast it. We're going to feast. We're going to have a wonderful time! My son is here- given up for dead and now alive! Given up for lost and now found!'*
>
> Luke 15:18-24 MSG

✎ **Describe in your own words the picture Jesus painted of the father who has waited for His son's return.**

_____

_____

_____

_____

_____

Amazingly, as Jesus tells this story the focus is not on the sinfulness of the son but on the generosity of the Father. The son had his speech carefully rehearsed; it was an elegant, polished statement of sorrow. But the Father didn't let him finish. God's love is so outrageous; He wants us back more than we want to be back.[42]

Like Kim, our greatest questions about God's unfairness can come to the surface when we encounter disappointment, wondering why God allowed the pain, sorrow, or trials.

✎ **Write about a time you were disappointed with a situation or with God.**

_____

_____

_____

_____

_____

Philip Yancey's _Disappointment with God_ helps us confront those questionings and shows us how we have confused the fairness of life with God:

Life should be fair because God is fair. But God is not life....The Son of God reacted to life's unfairness much like anybody else. When he met a person in pain, he was deeply moved with compassion. When his friend Lazarus died, he wept. When Jesus himself faced suffering, he recoiled from it, asking three times if there was another way.[43]

Yancey's central point is that God and life are not the same. If life was fair, Christ who was without sin would not have had to go to the cross for us. **Because we live in a fallen world, none of us are exempt from unfairness.** The cross of Christ overcame evil but not unfairness. Once we clarify that in our minds, we are able to see the real enemy and how to deal with the bondage in which we find ourselves.

We know the enemy Satan would love to keep us in bondage. But what is the way out? Kim's confession of needing God is a great start. She was recognizing that she was powerless over her behavior and that trying harder wasn't working. What does work? How do we come to freedom?

Paul rehearses our dilemma in Romans 7: *I don't understand myself at all, for I really want to do what is right but I can't. I do what I don't want to —what I hate.* (Romans 7:15 Living Bible)

Paul answers this dilemma in Romans 12. *"And do not be conformed to this world; but be transformed by the renewing of your mind."* (Romans 12:2 NKJ)

In the Bible, the New Testament is vividly clear:

The Battlefield of Your Life Is In Your Mind!

We will be talking about two parts of the brain that comprise most of the battlefield Paul is referring to in Romans: The Prefrontal Cortex and the Limbic or survival part of the brain.

Prefrontal Cortex: Starting up front is the **Frontal Lobe** and specifically the **Prefrontal Cortex;** this is the arena of your working memory and concentration.[44]

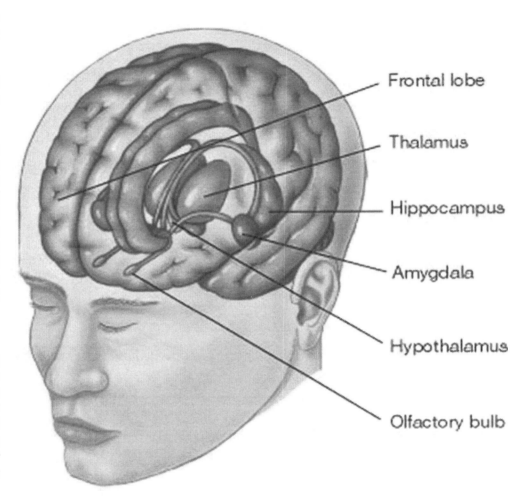

Frontal lobe

Thalamus

Hippocampus

Amygdala

Hypothalamus

Olfactory bulb

This is where executive planning and social awareness and impulse control take place. This area of your brain shuts down when you are compulsively acting out. I will tell how and why later on.

Your brain also doesn't come fully programmed, which is one of its great strengths because of its infinite adaptability. The brain usually isn't fully developed until your mid-twenties. Specifically, your Prefrontal Cortex isn't fully matured until then, which means impulse control and judgment can be lacking. For that reason, car rental businesses require you to be 26 before you can rent a car. We will get back to the importance of that with respect to sexual bondage in just a moment.

By touring the part of the brain known as the limbic system or survival brain, which is fully developed by age six, we can see why we, like Kim, get stuck in the Romans 7 dilemma.

Limbic System: This is comprised of the amygdala, hippocampus, and medial thalamus.[45] The amygdala is focused solely on survival. It is your early-warning system. It processes information even before the prefrontal cortex gets the message that something has happened. When you smile at the sight or sound of someone you love even before you consciously recognize the person, the amygdala is at work. The amygdala defines what you see as being critical for your survival. It underlines in your memory what you should flee from or what you are willing to fight for so you can survive. It also underlines what is so terrifying to you that you will just freeze, rendering you unable to respond to the threat. **The amygdala defines what food is critical for your survival and what is vital for you sexually.**

An essential feature of brain anatomy is the fact that there are more connections running from the amygdala to the cortex than the other way around. **This means the amygdala will win the battle every time.** That is why Paul is in such despair in Romans 7. When these two parts of your brain are at war with one another, it is a bit like Mike Tyson facing off with Napoleon Dynamite. Fear, anger, and sexual desire, which all stem from the amygdala, are notoriously resistant to our ability to reason ourselves out of them. Once fearful reactions or traumatic memories (especially sexual ones) are burned into the amygdala, they tend to lock the mind and body into a recurring pattern of arousal. We have a great deal of difficulty restraining an excited amygdala. Mike Tyson will win every time.

Remember Cindy in the basement with her boyfriend? Her prefrontal cortex shut down when things got hot and heavy. Her logical brain telling her she did not want to have sex could not overpower her survival brain telling her she needed affection from a man. Her need to be held by her daddy when she was three is a survival need Cindy was trying to meet through other means.

In the struggle with sexual desire, your prefrontal cortex commitment to Christ is usually being pulled off course by the subconscious decision of your limbic system deep within your brain. When you continue to make choices that don't make any sense in your life, when you repeatedly make destructive sexual decisions, mark it down *as a Limbic System problem.*

 ✎ **Share about a time when you realize now that you were fighting against your limbic system.**

_____

_____

_____

_____

We will be looking more at the limbic system in future chapters, but for now we want to share a simple tool that will help you begin to reprogram your limbic or survival brain.

Like Kim and Cindy, you may be unaware of how you end up doing the very thing you didn't want to do. That is where your new journey begins. The only way to change directions is to become self-aware of the slippery steps you have unconsciously taken that have led you in the wrong direction—to the pit of relapse.

To reach a new destination, we need to break down the big picture of our lives into smaller scenes of decision-making. These smaller decisions can alter the direction of our lives, steering us into becoming joyful, fruitful, healthy young women rather than lonely, needy, and hopelessly stuck in bondage. With Christ advocating for you and God smiling on you, every step you take towards healing and wholeness will be blessed!

The **FASTER Relapse Awareness Scale**, created by Michael Dye as part of *The Genesis Process*,[46] is a tool that helps us break down the process that causes us to slip and slide into relapse. The FASTER scale helps us see how unwise decisions increase our isolation and neglect of ourselves. The scale helps us pinpoint how we medicate our pain, falling back into bondage. We will learn to stop the process and get back on the track toward healing. This is good news! We are not destined to repeat our mistakes and live in misery!

Most of us aren't consciously aware of how we end in the pit of relapse. Yet Scripture admonishes us in Romans: *But put on the Lord Jesus Christ, and make no **provision** of the flesh, to fulfill its lusts.* (Romans 13:14 NKJ)

The word for provision means fore-planning, foresight, premeditated plan. In order to make no provision for the flesh, it is important to be aware of the unconscious steps our minds have taken in the past.

The following diagram will help you discover those steps leading to the downward spiral of acting out. As shown, the steps toward the top have more room for your feet but those steps at the bottom are very difficult to get your toe onto, let alone have a good grip. Imagine that these steps are also wet and slippery due to the storms of life, and it isn't hard to understand how you can quickly slip into the pit again.[47]

Restoration/Recovery

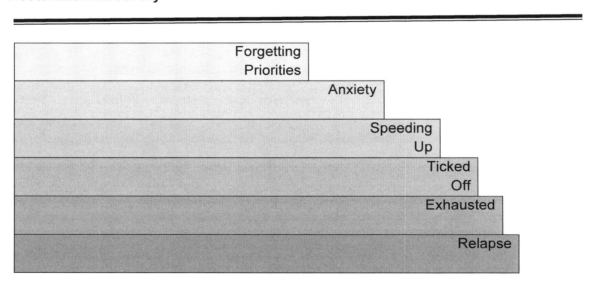

The best news about this is that anytime you find yourself slipping down this progressively dangerous scale, you don't have to crawl back up one step at a time. For instance, if you catch yourself feeling really angry and you want to make improvements, you don't have to move up the scale to speeding up, then being anxious, then forgetting priorities until you reach restoration. Confront yourself and focus again on what is truly beneficial. Real breakthrough can come when you face the dilemmas head on, bringing them to light and finding solutions that may be hard but are the right thing to do.

For processing specific dilemmas on the steps of the scale, the **Double Bind** exercise tool will help you look at options and choose a path of action towards health.[48] A double bind is a difficult place in which you feel like you can't win with any of the choices available to you. The problems don't go away but intensify, thus making your internal conflicts greater. At this point, you usually slip quickly down the FASTER scale towards relapse. Facing the fear and doing the hard thing is the best path for finding resolution from your turmoil.

Look at the following examples for a better understanding of how to use the **Double Bind** tool.

CHOICES			APPLY FORMULA	PLAN
Problem/ Situation	If I do change & believe what God says about me [face the problem]	If I don't change & continue viewing myself as I have in the past [avoid the problem]	The Right Thing is usually the Hard Thing	Plan to change: What, When, Who, Where, and How?
I isolate and then fantasy begins to consume me and I call a guy from school and we hook-up.	I'll have to face the fear of being alone & why I avoid support from God & others. I'll also have to face the pain I've been medicating with fantasy & eventual acting-out.	I will continue to avoid support and spiral downward into making unhealthy choices and end up relapsing.	Journal about why I am isolating and immediately contact a close friend to process the reason for my isolation.	Journal concerns immediately and call two of my support group friends. Schedule a time to go to coffee to break the isolation pattern.
Feel panicked and stressed over school deadlines I have put off because I am afraid of failure. I want to numb out by cutting or masturbating.	I will need to face my fear of failure, plan out my time and schedule time for the school project even if it doesn't turn out perfect.	Without a plan the stress will lead to physical symptoms of fatigue/ anxiety, and I will end up cutting or masturbating again.	Journal about my fear of failure and why I need to be perfect. Discuss with friends my stress and have them pray for me.	I will ask a school friend to help me make a calendar schedule with due dates and be accountable to her. I will let my parents know about the cutting and be willing to get counseling
Became friends on Facebook with a guy from school and we have been talking sexually. I fantasize being with him sexually.	I need to address the fantasies, share this with my accountability partners and have my parents help with the solution.	I'll continue to fantasize, keep our dialogues going on Facebook and feed into a possible scenario of acting out with this guy.	I must share this with my small group and journal so the secret won't eat at me. I will confess this to my parents and discontinue any dialogues with this guy.	I will talk to my accountability group tonight. I will drop this guy from my Facebook; I will give my parents access to my Facebook page and all my correspondence.

Michael Dye's FASTER Relapse Awareness Scale appears on the next page. Following the chart is a discussion that focuses on the scale as it is used in the Pure Desire for Women classes.

FASTER Relapse Awareness Scale

Adapted from the Genesis Process by Michael Dye (used by permission)
www.genesisprocess.org

<u>Recovery/Restoration</u> – (**Accepting life on God's terms, with trust, grace, mercy, vulnerability and gratitude.**) No current secrets; working to resolve problems; identifying fears and feelings; keeping commitments to meetings, prayer, family, church, people, goals, and self; being open and honest, making eye contact; increasing in relationships with God and others; true accountability.

<u>Forgetting Priorities</u> - (**Start believing the present circumstances and moving away from trusting God. Denial, flight, a change in what's important; how you spend your time, energy, and thoughts.**) Secrets; less time/energy for God, meetings, church; avoiding support and accountability people; superficial conversations; sarcasm; isolating; changes in goals; obsessed with relationships; breaking promises & commitments; neglecting family; preoccupation with material things, T.V., computers, entertainment; procrastination; lying; over-confidence; bored; hiding money.

Forgetting priorities will lead to:

<u>A</u>nxiety – (**A growing background noise of undefined fear; getting energy from emotions.**) Worry, using profanity, being fearful; being resentful; replaying old, negative thoughts; perfectionism; judging other's motives; making goals and lists that you can't complete; mind reading; fantasy, co-dependent rescuing; sleep problems, trouble concentrating, seeking/creating drama; gossip; using over-the-counter medication for pain, sleep or weight control; flirting.

Anxiety then leads to:

<u>S</u>peeding Up – (**Trying to outrun the anxiety which is usually the first sign of depression.**) Super busy and always in a hurry (finding good reason to justify the work), workaholic, can't relax; avoiding slowing down; feeling driven; can't turn off thoughts; skipping meals; binge eating (usually at night); overspending; can't identify own feelings/needs; repetitive negative thoughts; irritable; dramatic mood swings; too much caffeine; over exercising; nervousness; difficulty being alone and/or with people; difficulty listening to others; making excuses for having to "do it all."

Speeding up then leads to:

<u>T</u>icked Off – (**Getting adrenaline high on anger and aggression.**) Procrastination causing crisis in money, work, and relationships; increased sarcasm; black and white (all or nothing) thinking; feeling alone; nobody understands; overreacting, road rage; constant resentments; pushing others away; increasing isolation; blaming; arguing; irrational thinking; can't take criticism; defensive; people avoiding you; needing to be right; digestive problems; headaches; obsessive (stuck) thoughts; can't forgive; feeling superior; using intimidation.

Ticked off then leads to:

<u>E</u>xhausted – (**Loss of physical and emotional energy; coming off the adrenaline high, and the onset of depression.**) Depressed; panicked; confused; hopelessness; sleeping too much or too little; can't cope; overwhelmed; crying for "no reason"; can't think; forgetful; pessimistic; helpless; tired; numb; wanting to run; constant cravings for old coping behaviors, thinking of using sex, drugs, or alcohol; seeking old unhealthy people & places; really isolating; people angry with you; self-abuse; suicidal thoughts; spontaneous crying; no goals; survival mode; not returning phone calls; missing work, irritability; no appetite.

Exhausted then leads to:

<u>R</u>elapse/Moral Failure – (**Returning to the place you swore you would never go again. Coping with life on your terms. You sitting in the driver's seat instead of God.**) Giving up and giving in; out of control; lost in your addiction; lying to yourself and others; feeling you just can't manage without your coping behaviors, at least for now. The result is the reinforcement of shame, guilt and condemnation; and feelings of abandonment and being alone.

66 | Behind the Mask: Authentic Living for Young Women

At the point of relapse, we know we are absolutely spent and hopeless. The bondage has gained control of us, whether it is pornography and masturbation, hooking up, sexting, computer sex, etc. These are endless pits that destroy your soul and only you thoroughly know your specific behaviors that lead to relapse.

∾ **Review each category on the FASTER Scale and highlight or circle the words or phrases with which you can most identify, now or in your past.**

∾ **Which word or phrase under the <u>Relapse</u> category is the most powerful behavior for you?**

∾ **What effect does this behavior have on you?**

_____

_____

_____

_____

∾ **How does this behavior affect your relationships?**

_____

_____

_____

_____

∾ **What are the benefits of choosing this behavior? What motivates you to keep doing it?**

_____

_____

_____

_____

∾ Now do a Double Bind using the most serious or dangerous situation on which you need to focus. (It may be helpful to use the previous Double Bind example to help you discover your own Double Bind.) Be prepared to share your Double Bind with your group.

CHOICES			APPLY FORMULA	PLAN
Problem/ Situation	If I do change & believe what God says about me [face the problem]	If I don't change & continue viewing myself as I have in the past [avoid the problem]	The Right Thing is usually the Hard Thing	Plan to change: What, When, Who, Where, and How?

Accountability

Invite one or two people to help you be accountable for your FASTER Scale or Double Bind commitments. Your accountability partners might be from your *Behind the Mask* group or trusted friends or adults.

Look at Kim's Accountability Card example. She transferred what was highlighted on her FASTER Scale to a card that helps her look at a glance at her struggles. She is able to identify Old Behaviors that she wants to stop and New Behaviors she wants to start.

Name: Kim	Contact Info: home 503-555-5555; cell 503-555-5555

Triggers/Relapse Behaviors

F Isolating/avoiding support; easy to get preoccupied
A Replaying old negative thoughts; fantasy
S Too much caffeine, think about ways we could hook-up
T Feeling alone and needy and obsessive
E Becoming overwhelmed, skipping school
R Falling apart emotionally; acting out sexually when he initiates contact

Old Behaviors	New Behaviors
Not answering my phone when friends call	Picking up phone when friends call
Fantasy & obsessive thinking	Journal instead of fantasying
Avoiding prayer & time with God	20 min. with God daily at 7 a.m.
Isolating; avoiding support	Lunch with friend once a week

❧ **Transfer some of your FASTER Scale information from this lesson to note cards to share with others in your small group; this will enhance accountability.**

- Fill in your 2 or 3 most common behaviors for each step in the FASTER Scale. The more personalized you make your card, the more enlightening and helpful it will be to you and the others you invite to hold you accountable.

- Make copies to give to each person you ask to be an accountability partner, as well as one to keep for yourself.

- Bring these cards with you to your next *Behind the Mask* group meeting.

Accountability Card	
Name:	Contact Info:

Triggers/Relapse Behaviors
F
A
S
T
E
R

Old Behaviors	New Behaviors

Accountability Card & FASTER Scale are tools from the Genesis Change Process, www.genesisprocess.org. Used by permission.

Assignments

1. Ask yourself daily, "Where am I on the FASTER scale today?"

2. Decide who you will invite to be your accountability partners and prepare Accountability Cards for them.

> Song recommendation for meditation this week:
> **Beautiful**
> by Mercy Me

3. Be prepared to share the most serious or dangerous Double Bind on which you need to focus.

4. Complete the next chapter.

Daring to Be Real

Chapter 6
The Pain Behind the Mask

"When someone shows grace to us, that person begins cultivating an environment that reflects God's grace. It is an authentic, unhidden place where our masks start melting, our sin can be known and therefore addressed with power and grace." [49]

Jessica

I am lying on my back. My body is safe and unashamed in a huge open field of grass and wildflowers, my arms spread open. The sun covers me like a blanket with its warmth. I am at peace. The breeze wafts the light and airy fragrance of lilies through my nose, tickling my senses. I am alive. The masks that I have been hiding behind have melted back into my heart, from where I built them. I am finally free.

In my chest there is pain, but I feel an overwhelming sense of safety and security. I look down to see what hurts, and I see my wound. My gaping wound. In fact, I am in open-heart surgery, right there in the field. My entire chest has been surgically opened and my insides are bloody and exposed. Searing pain shoots throughout my body, like a shock to my system. Then, I look up and see my surgeon. I am safe again. My breathing returns to normal. It is Him. My Savior, my King, leaning over me and tenderly inspecting my insides, the insides He created. The look on His face shows concern but also hope. He knows what needs to happen next.

Why must I face this pain again? In my mind I willed the surgery to go faster. I imagined my wounds closing on the spot. My chest would close magically and I would rise to go somewhere else, anywhere but here. Here is extremely uncomfortable. Here is painful. Here is intimacy with a God I am only learning to trust again.

I look at His face again. Beautiful. Trustworthy. He was the One who saw behind my masks in the first place. And He was the one who loved me just the same, even though He knew what I had done. The Lord is not scared by the state of my insides as He works; He is just so loving as He massages my heart. He is patient with me. He heals me at His own pace. So here I am. Wounded, but completely aware of my pain. Trusting in the Lord once again, I am trusting Him with my pain as well.

I settle back into the green grass and keep my eyes on Him. I breathe in His sweet presence strong and deeply. I must look outside of me during this life to find peace. Rest comes from my God alone.

We have all been through pain. In this chapter you will read the stories of painful moments, the roots of the issues. Now is the time we get to look at the source of our compulsive behavior. Let's take it back to the beginning.

Anna

The pattern in the musty carpet moved in and out of focus as I stared it down. The bed sheets felt stiff and reeked of the alcohol that had been on his breath. The pit of my stomach twisted into solid steel. I felt a trail of warm blood drip down my legs onto the coarse bed. My mind had escaped, but my fragile body was still there, refusing to move from the fetal position. What was wrong with me that someone would treat me this way?

He came back into the room, this time holding a gun. I froze. He grabbed my hair, forcing me to sit up on the bed. He gripped my hair in one hand and yanked it towards him. With the other hand, he held the gun to my head and whispered the words that seared into my mind, "You tell anyone about this, and I will kill you. You WILL die if anyone else knows. Do you understand me?" I nodded quickly; he threw me back onto the bed. This wasn't the first time I had been raped, and if I could see the future, I would know that it would not be last. My abuser stole my innocence, my virginity, and my hope of ever feeling safe again.

I try to escape these memories, but my body cannot forget. I still have nightmares of the fear, the pain, the disabling experience. I was 11 when my mom's boyfriend raped me. He repeatedly tortured me like this for two more years. Each time my mother planned to leave, I begged her not to leave my sisters and me alone. Being the oldest daughter, I was not only scared for myself, but for my sisters' safety. Sometimes we would hide in the closet, lock the doors for hours until her boyfriend left. My mom, a meth addict, often went to parties, leaving us alone with complete strangers. She still, to this day, refuses to believe what happened to me. I understand some of that; I did not want to believe it either. For weeks I kept quiet, until I could not stop the churning inside me.

Finally, I sought comfort in the arms of my dad. I told him the truth about what had happened at my mother's house. My already fractured heart was shattered by what happened next: he refused to believe me. The mother who was supposed to protect me had betrayed me, and now my dad, whom I had trusted, accused me of lying. I had already been abandoned by my mom who chose drugs over me, and now I was emotionally abandoned by my dad in my time of greatest need. Constantly I felt as if I were suffocating, drowning in my own life. How does anyone continue to live after that? I had no one to heal my unworthy heart, and I was not strong enough to heal myself. My mind did everything it could to stuff the hurt and memories inside my body so that I could at least get out of bed each day.

Shutting out the memories of my abuse helped me function: go to school, eat, shop, put a smile on my face. But in reality the hurt swelled inside of me. Eventually this pain got too much for even my body to handle. I needed out, but had no way to process this. Using razor blades, I started cutting my wrists. Cutting masked the emotional pain and opened up a part of me so that I could see I was alive. Cutting helped me feel normal again, even if it were for only a moment.

I find myself today in patterns of lying and doing things for guys even though I do not want to. It's like I can't help it. This trauma from my past has changed me in ways I am struggling to reclaim. I want to trust men, but I tend to react out of fear instead of confidence or strength.

❧ What was Anna's limbic response to her abuser's gun held to her head?

Fight? Flight? Freeze? _____

<s> **How did she cope with her pain?**

_____

_____

Today, Anna is right where you are. She is a young woman at the beginning of her healing process. She is working through identifying and coming to terms with what happened to her, understanding how her abuse has affected the way she relates to others, and letting the Holy Spirit into her life on a daily basis as she works through the reactions and responses set in her brain.

<s> **Anna was violated and abused in several different ways. Do you relate to any of the ways she was abused? If so, share below:**

_____

_____

_____

Overall, Anna's story is filled with pain that has shaped the way she deals with life. Perhaps you also have hurt that has shaped how you face life. If you could relate to this story, you are a survivor. You did not give up and die, but you made it through and are pressing forward. You are a hero. We will continue to explore Anna's trauma and unmask your own story in the pages that follow.

Jessica

I lived in a box my entire life and didn't even know it.

My box was three feet high. Someone had hammered together particleboard and painted it black on the inside and the outside. Emotionally, this was my home. Sometime during my childhood I had crouched inside. The lid was closed and darkness slid all around me, except for a one-inch hole from which I could peer out.

I wanted out, but a force I could not name held me back. Something deep within me knew that if I stepped out, I would not know who I was. My identity was trapped by the restrictions that others made for me.

Lies I rehearsed in my head haunted every choice I made: "I won't get love unless I do what they tell me to do. It makes others angry and disappointed when I fail. I cannot fail, or they will not love me." The only way I thought I could be happy was by fitting squarely into the box.

Behind every decision I made, the voices continued: "I am not good enough. I wish I were different. Why can't I be more like someone else? I am not capable on my own. In this box I find safety because they make my decisions for me. I am no good on my own.   God will not love me if I do not obey them. If I reach the expectations of others, then I might have a fighting chance to feel worth something. Maybe then I can be valued."

And so I remained, in that hypothetical box for most of my life. My mind was constantly on guard, stressed out, and anxious. I wanted to be loved, but felt alone and unlovable. I felt like I needed my parents' love more than I needed to be myself. However, I did not believe them *when they spoke love from their mouths. I thought I had gained their approval by what I did, but I feared they would reject me if they knew I was imperfect. I was kept in line by their looks of disapproval when I tried to pry the box open. Throughout those years, sermons on purity poured over me like bleach; sin must be removed and I cannot be around it. This shaped my friends, my worldview, and my view of how God sees me. I heard about grace, but rarely felt it. I hated myself. I could never measure up.*

I never doubted that love was conditional and gifts had strings attached to them. I could have friends if my parents knew everything about them and approved. I could date if my family approved and if I lived in between their lines. I got smiles if I performed well. I felt ashamed if I did not live like they would. Their intentions were good, but I perceived their actions as judging me. I do not remember many conversations with my mom where I came away feeling better about myself. When she suggested a different way of doing things, I interpreted it as her not accepting the decisions I was making. I became insecure and felt inadequate. All of my choices were made on the basis of whether or not I would be loved by what I did. Even subconsciously I heard my parents' voices over my own. My own unique voice became very small, and hid in the back of my mind until very recently. I reverted to acting about 12 years old when I was around them, even though I had moved to college. I did not mature emotionally at a healthy rate.

At times we, like Jessica, have all felt like we have been trapped inside some type of box. Sometimes it is a box of our own making. It may be a box that protects us from an unsafe environment.

✎ **Draw your box with labels that show the things you think imprisoned you.**

Perhaps you have faced emotional and verbal abuse like Jessica. Perhaps the abuse you have faced is more tangible like Anna's story. Maybe you were physically or sexually abused. Maybe you don't recognize the abuse that you faced, or have never thought of it as abuse. **Until you see yourself and take off your own masks, you will continue walking through life in unhealthy patterns, frustrating yourself, and perhaps even harming yourself or those around you.**

Sometimes people may believe removing their masks will reveal only ugliness and fear, and that increases their fear of knowing their true self. However, when that fear is faced, the mask can melt away, and you can see how God sees you, as His precious daughter who has been completely saved and completely washed clean in forgiveness. Nothing is more beautiful than the face of one redeemed by the grace of God.

Your trauma story

❧ **To which of these two stories do you most relate? Why?**

_____

_____

_____

Each of these true stories contains trauma; some came in what I call the form of a "whack" and some in the form of "lack." The whack is abuse that is tangible: a slap to the face, rape, or sexual assault like Anna experienced. Sometimes the abuse is subtle, such as name-calling, criticism, or rigid demands that require you fit into a predetermined mold. Lack is the absence of something good. Jessica had emotional abuse that came from living in a home absent of safety. She never had a safe place to develop into a woman. Anna experienced lack when she was denied her basic needs of love and safety.

Scripture helps us understand how the whacks and lacks of our past can cripple us in the present. Let's look at an example from the Old Testament.

> *Saul's son Jonathan had a son named Mephibosheth, who was crippled as a child. He was five years old when the report came from Jezreel that Saul and Jonathan had been killed in battle. When the child's nurse heard the news, she picked him up and fled. But as she hurried away, she dropped him, and he became crippled.*
> 2 Samuel 4:4 (NLT)

The news that David had become the new king spread like a violent shockwave throughout Israel. And it was terrifying news to the household of Saul for this reason: it was Standard Operating Procedure for a new unknown king to hunt down and butcher every member of the previous king's family. If he didn't, they could rise up against him and reclaim the throne. Mephibosheth's nurse didn't know David's heart so she ran for her life in panic. In her haste to save herself, she dropped the child and as a result he was crippled in both feet. Therefore, the reason Mephibosheth is struggling now is because someone dropped him in the past.[50]

Some of the compulsive behaviors and struggles you have now are because someone has dropped you in your past. Someone you were counting on to be responsible and supportive dropped you. You have survived, but, like Mephibosheth, you walk with a limp; what happened in your past affects your walk in the present.

The compulsive behavior you may be struggling with today is a means of dealing with the crippling effect of your past. For that reason we want to look at trauma from your past. It is painful to look under the mask of hidden hurts, but with God's help and the encouragement of your group, healing will come.

All of us have some hurts in our lives; that is part of living in a fallen world. As you can see from the following charts, past hurts come in two forms: "whack"—with high or low intensity and/or "lack" with high to low intensity. Often, small hurts are repeated over and over, which can lead to higher intensity. Both kinds of trauma and past hurts can lead to compulsive behaviors in attempts to medicate the pain.

- ❧ **Note the examples in each category of "whacks" and "lacks" and then add some examples from your life.** Since each person might categorize intensity depending on her own experiences, don't limit yourself by the examples given. You may want to read through the "Wounded Heart" section before completing the "WHACKS" and "LACKS" charts.

WHACKS

High Intensity
Examples:
- Parents divorce
- Death of someone close to you
- Sexual abuse
- Abuse by an older sibling
- Many losses of close friends
- On-going physical & emotional abuse

My examples:

Medium Intensity
Examples:
- Some physical or emotional abuse
- Being bullied

My examples:

Low Intensity
Examples:
- Name-calling
- Feeling devalued/ not heard
- Loss of best friend

My examples:

LACKS

High Intensity
Examples:
- Abandoned by 1 or both parents
- Parent loses job which leads to lack of financial resources

My examples:

Medium Intensity
Examples:
- Parents ignore your input or needs
- Older sibling won't have anything to do with you
- Moved frequently/hard to find new friends
- No validation of achievements

My examples:

Low Intensity
Examples:
- Very little validation of efforts or achievements by parents or others

My examples:

Your Wounded Heart

❧ **Draw pictures in the heart that follows, using these instructions:**

Bottom third. Think of your earliest memories of a whack or lack that devalued you as a child. In the bottom third, draw pictures of past hurts that happened before the age of six. They can represent small or intense hurts. Anna might draw her mom, waving goodbye as she left her family behind. Jessica would draw her dad with eyebrows furrowed, looking down at her.

Middle third. Draw pictures that represent your pre-teen years. Anna could draw a picture of her dad covering his ears, not willing to listen to her pain. Jessica would draw a piece of duct tape covering her own mouth, representing her own voice being cut off.

Top third. Create pictures that represent your teen years to present age. As a teen, Anna might draw a razor showing how she has coped with the pain, which is also trauma. Jessica might draw a ruler showing how she has tried to measure up to outward expectations.

My Wounded Heart

❧ **Look over the pictures you drew of your past hurts. What messages were communicated to you because of the whacks or lacks in your life?**

Examples: I am damaged goods; those closest to me always abandon me; life is not safe.

1 _____

2 _____

3 _____

4 _____

5 _____

We can allow trauma to define us and try to cover that trauma with masks or we can hear the truth of who God says we are. God never defines us according to our past hurts, but sees behind the mask and sees our true heart.

That is what happened to Mephibosheth. Years had passed and King David asks if there are any people left in the house of Saul whom he can bless. When his servant found Mephibosheth, this is what David communicates to him:

"Do not fear, for I will surely show you kindness....and will restore to you all the land of Saul your grandfather; and you shall eat bread at my table." 2 Samuel 9:7 NKJ

David knew Mephibosheth's rightful place was at the king's table and restored what was lost. Jesus has that for you also.

❧ **Rather than seeing yourself as being crippled, discover how Jesus sees you. Look in the back of this book under Resources and find the page titled, "Who I Am In Christ." Find five statements from Scripture that counter the messages communicated to you by your whacks and lacks.**

1 _____

2 _____

3 _____

4 _____

5 _____

Daily rehearsing the statements above will help you begin to see yourself as the King's daughter seated at His table, restored to your rightful place of honor before Him.

As you meditate on these scriptures, ask God to give you a new picture of how He sees you. Draw that picture in the space provided. Be ready to share that picture with your group.

Look at your God-given picture every night this week before you go to bed. Pray that the Lord will show you the broken places He wants to heal.

Think of a double bind you face if you are willing to act on who God says you are.

Review the example and then complete your double bind using the form that follows.

Example:

CHOICES				PLAN
Problem/ Situation	If I do change & believe what God says about me (face the problem)	If I don't change & continue viewing myself as I have in the past (avoid the problem)	The Right Thing is the Hard Thing	Plan to change
Have looked at myself as a victim & have felt I deserve to be mistreated by guys	I am God's precious daughter who deserves to be treated with respect; I will have to face the fear of setting healthy boundaries & treating myself with respect. I will have to face the possibility of rejection by guys.	I will let others treat me with disrespect & will have to continue wearing a mask and feeling like a victim.		1. Every night I will rehearse the Scriptures that declare who I am. 2. By Chapter 13, I will have healthy boundaries in place & have 2 accountability partners. 3. I will monitor myself daily on FASTER Scale for victim mentality behaviors.

My Double Bind:

	CHOICES			PLAN
Problem/ Situation	If I do change & believe what God says about me (face the problem)	If I don't change & continue viewing myself as I have in the past (avoid the problem)	The Right Thing is the Hard Thing	Plan to change

Additional suggestions for those who have been abused

Anna had flashbacks, both visual and physical. Sometimes she would get a "sense" in her muscles of the night she was raped. When she was abused, her young brain could not process that pain, so it actually stored those memories in her body. The flashbacks would come at unexpected times and, along with her nightmares, could last for weeks. If you have experienced flashbacks regarding a traumatic event, here are techniques that other survivors of sexual abuse have found helpful:

1. Ask yourself, "What am I feeling in my emotions?" By identifying your emotions, you can separate the flashback from your present experiences.

2. Ask yourself, "What am I feeling in my physical being, in my body?" One survivor could feel her dad's hands choking her neck. Identifying what she was sensing helped her grasp what was happening to her in the present.

3. Ask yourself, "Is it the anniversary of something?" Anna had flashbacks around the same season every year—around Halloween, when she had first been raped. Identifying timelines can help you understand the trigger of the flashback.

4. Finally, tell a safe person that you are having the flashbacks. Sometimes, giving voice to what you are going through takes the power away from the abuser in your head. You have the power now because you have a voice and are using it. The voice of most sexual abuse survivors was taken from them during the abuse. Telling someone else reclaims that voice and may help in shortening the flashback.

5. If the flashbacks continue, please seek professional help. This is an issue with how your brain is dealing with trauma, not simply something that will go away by trying harder.

℣ As you listen to the song recommended here, *consider the source of pain for the girls singing this song. Be prepared to discuss this with your group next time you meet.*

Song recommendations for meditation this week:
I Feel Pretty/Unpretty
by Glee Season Two

———

Remind Me Who I Am
by Jason Gray

Chapter 7
Seeing Your Present Reality in Light of your Past

If Anna and Jessica completed the Post-Traumatic Stress Index (PTSI) that is included in this book, their scores would be high in many areas. They would have the opportunity to realize God had been working in their lives, but now with these PTSI scores they could see specific indicators of where more healing needs to take place.

Stop now and take the PTSI evaluation[51] in the Resources section at the end of this book, making sure you tally the scores on the Stress Index Answer Grid.

After completing the PTSI you are probably interested in understanding what your scores mean. Before we look at your specific scores in the first six columns of the Answer Grid, it is critical that we have a biblical context in which to interpret them.[52]

If your score was three or higher in any of the first six categories of the PTSI you are carrying a lot of pain in life. Joseph, a character in the Old Testament, also had a lot of pain in his life. Perhaps you can relate. Let's walk through the background of the story.

Facing the fear of seeing behind my mask

In Genesis 15, God declared to Abraham that his children would go into a strange land where they would be enslaved for 400 years. Yet, He would bring them out of the land of bondage with great wealth. He basically told the Israelites, "I am going to take you to a place you have never been in your life. You are going to be there awhile. **When I bring you out, you are going to come out with more than you had before you went in.**" That is exactly where God is taking you as you walk through your healing journey.

Abraham died before he saw the fulfillment of that word. God could have just forgotten that promise but that would have been totally counter to His character. He kept His promise to Abraham...a dead man. Just think how much more God is going to keep His word to you. Someone committed to His Son, someone who is alive and waiting on Him. God is sovereign and He has a strategy for your life. The first thing you need to know about your Sovereign God is ...

He will keep His word to you no matter what your PTSI scores are!

The Bible tells us that when a famine broke out in the land, Abraham's children were forced to move to Egypt. Because of the abuse and betrayal at the hands of his brothers, Joseph had already been strategically placed in the land as a forerunner for the family. Now stop and think about that for a moment. God didn't cause the dysfunctional craziness of Joseph's family, but He used their mistreatment of Joseph for His sovereign purposes.

God is so strategic that He even uses adversity to maneuver or position you into the right place precisely at the right time. At times, you don't have a clue what is happening in your life. But down the road you will find yourself saying things like, "Lord, I am so glad I went through what I went through. It put me into the place you wanted me to be—a place of blessing." Or like Joseph, **"What they meant for evil you made into good."** (Genesis 50:20)

As you look at your PTSI scores in light of the healing that God is bringing into your life, you will realize an incredible truth. **God will even use adversity to position you for blessing…if you let Him!**

You might ask, "So, how do I let Him do that?" There is another critical piece to the puzzle that is the most frustrating piece. **God will not always give you the details of how things are working out for your blessing.** For example, God told Abraham his children were going to be enslaved in Egypt but He didn't say a word about:

> … the famine.

> … one of his great-grandchildren who would be sold into slavery by his own family.

> … his great-grandson who would be abused by his own brothers and end up a jail bird.

> … how the imprisonment that this same heir would experience would suddenly catapult him into a position of incredible prominence and power!

Don't miss the fact that Joseph didn't become the prince of Egypt without going through betrayal and injustice, without maxing out his PTSI scores. Many a speaker has said, "All you have to do is just believe the promises of God. Just plant the seed. Just believe God and you will get 'it'," whatever the 'it' may be. Such statements are the "religious slot machine" approach; put the correct prayer or religious activity *in* and your blessing will come *out*. However, you will never find a simple blessing story like that in Scripture.

When God builds a Christian's life, He will use the pain of the world to accomplish His sovereign shaping purposes. Strong believers always create the foundations for their lives from the stones that others have thrown at them.

🔊 **What stones have others thrown at you?**

_____

_____

In practice, to say that God is sovereign means He will do a lot of things you don't understand. At times, that truth will deeply upset you and make you fearful. The answer to this dilemma is realizing that the promises of God and perils of your life usually go together. But don't let that intimidate you; it is part of the process. The peril will lead you to the promise if you trust God.

Joseph was betrayed three times and yet this pain and agony he experienced at the hands of his brothers and others in Egypt was used by the sovereign hand of God. This whole process enabled God's man to be in high places to care for His people.

That is a fascinating picture of what God can do in your life. Many young women going through the healing process have not only found their own healing, but also have been there for other young women who have been devastated by their personal circumstances and history. In the midst of their own agony, they have seen God's plan for their life and how their troubles would bring blessing to other young women God cares about. You see, those PTSI scores are not just about you; they are about God's sovereign purposes in the lives of others as well.

In many ways, your trauma story might parallel that of the people of Israel who were beaten and abused by Pharaoh's taskmasters. **Research has revealed that 96% of those struggling with addictive behavior have been abused physically, sexually, and/or emotionally.**[53] The Israelites forgot God and worshipped the golden calf (Exodus 32). For us, abuse and trauma can subconsciously become reasons for medicating our pain, resulting in compulsive behavior. Like the Israelites, we, too, end up forgetting God and turn to worshiping unhealthy love relationships, sex, and other things.

  ❧ **How can you relate to these statistics in your own life?**

_____

_____

At times, you have probably found yourself thinking, "My behavior seems so illogical, especially when I love God with all my heart, and yet, here I am, bowing down before the idols of pleasing guys, masturbation, sexting, or _____." The truth is that all of us at some time or another can find ourselves bowing to idols like food, shopping, procrastination, control, perfectionism, substance abuse, and pleasing. When life seems overwhelming there are numerous options to medicate the trauma and pain within.

But here is the great news! **God never forgets you even when you try to forget Him!**

That is precisely why the more the Egyptians oppressed the Israelites, the more they grew. It is a strange thing about followers of the sovereign God: the more you oppress them, the greater their potential for growth. You see, when God really wants to grow you, He will allow an enemy to afflict you. That is why in every category where you scored three or higher in the PTSI, you are looking at a potential area of incredible breakthrough and growth in your life. The key is to not ignore the wound or obsess about it.

So what are the areas of potential breakthrough in your life? If you have not already done so, transfer your scores from the **PTSI Answer Grid** (at the end of the PTSI in the **Resources** section) to the corresponding boxes in this chapter. Note: We will only be using the first six scores on the Answer Grid (TRT, TR, TBD, TS, TP, and TB).

TRT...My Score _____

Trauma Reaction is an overall score indicating whether or not you are currently dealing with traumas from your past. The testimony of Jessica underlines her fears and TRT. She was reacting to being controlled by the demand for perfectionism in her family growing up.

Jessica lives with a high amount of anxiety in her life. Her trauma left an imprint on her brain with the false belief that she could not be worth anything unless she measured up to her parents' expectations. So, instead of waking up each morning believing she is a valuable person and capable to handle the world around her, she wakes up fearful of failing and incapable of making good decisions. In stressful situations, she has emotional breakdowns and anxiety attacks.

1. **If you scored 3 or more in this area, how do you react now to very difficult situations in your life?**

_____

_____

2. **What connection do you see between the way you react and the difficult distress of your past and present?**

_____

_____

_____

3. **Ask your friends to describe how you react at times in stressful, fearful or painful situations. List their responses below.**

_____

_____

_____

_____

Many young women find tremendous breakthrough by writing letters to abusive people of their past with the intention of setting healthy boundaries. These may or may not be sent. Remember, even as a young adult you can establish healthy boundaries that were impossible to set as a child. When you stop seeing yourself as a child, you will no longer stay stuck in your past.

4. **Thinking about your past abuse, who are some people to whom you might need to write letters?**

_____

_____

5. **Write one letter this week to one of the people identified in Question 4. (Note: This assignment involves writing a letter; the letter does not have to be sent.)**

TR... My Score _____

Trauma Repetition indicates whether or not you are repeating behaviors or situations that parallel early trauma experiences. As you may recall, Anna was raped and repeatedly abused by a man who had control over her body. She was trapped by the threat that she might be killed if she didn't comply. As she got older, Anna's life was no longer in danger but her survival brain responded as it did when she was younger. She still felt helplessly controlled in relationships with guys and tended to comply with their requests, even though she did not want to. For example, when Anna's ex-boyfriend asked for nude photos of her, she sent them even though it went against her beliefs.

Please remember: Processing our trauma stories is not intended to blame someone from the past, but to reclaim what was taken from us or not given to us. Anna's safety with men was compromised; the same survival reactions she developed in childhood are retained as she gets older.

1. **If you scored more than three in Trauma Repetition, describe how your history repeats itself in your life experiences.**

_____

_____

_____

_____

2. **What boundaries are you building in your life to avoid being triggered into Trauma Repetition? List them below.**

   Example: For Anna, she needed to find her voice and express new boundaries to those she dated. Also, Anna must recognize when she is triggered to comply with a man's request and give herself more time to process it longer, perhaps with safer females in her life, to make a safe choice for herself.

_____

_____

_____

3. **Intentional nurturing is essential for your healing. How are you caring for yourself in healthy ways?**

_____

_____

_____

4. **List at least one thing you can do to nurture yourself this week. Who will you ask to hold you accountable to do this?**

   Examples of nurturing yourself: Find a quiet place to listen to the recommended song from this chapter or one from a previous chapter that brought comfort to me; take a relaxing bath; go for a long walk; exercise; spend time on a craft, hobby or project that you enjoy.

   I will nurture myself by _____

   My accountability person is _____

TBD... My Score _____

Trauma Bonds indicate your vulnerability to be connected, loyal, and supportive to people who continue to shame or exploit you.

Jessica was raised in a home of criticism and sarcasm. Her mother would critique her appearance and her brother would make fun of her for little things he thought were funny. Jessica's dad responded to conversations with sarcastic remarks, which made intimacy impossible and prevented a meaningful relationship between them. To cope with the pain of feeling rejected and not measuring up, Jessica tried to meet all their expectations, but never could. In return, Jessica developed a shame-based loyalty to her family, out of fear of non-acceptance. She stood up for them at any cost and felt a deep need to defend their actions, views, and lifestyle to anyone who questioned it. In discussions with other people about her family, she always supported her parent's side of an argument and made decisions based on their views rather than being able to separate her identity from theirs. As an adult, Jessica still lived like that little girl, unable to detach from her parents. She felt incapable of living life on her own and afraid to think for herself lest she be rejected by her own family.

Another amazing story of TBD took place in 1973 in Stockholm, Sweden. Two bank robbers held, threatened, and abused hostages during a five-and-a-half day siege. The hostage-takers told authorities that if their demands were not met, they would kill the hostages. The hostages were abused at times, but also treated with kindness by being given food and water. The hostages were told of their abductors' cause to free friends who were at that point in prison. In essence, through intense fear, high trauma, and the facade of intimacy, the captives bonded strongly to the bank robbers. Some captives even sought to protect the abductors from harsh treatment by the police, giving the robbers hugs and kisses at their departures. One female captive became a good friend of one of the captors. Another captive raised legal defense funds to obtain the captors' release. Trauma bonds can be formed almost instantaneously (in this case five-and-a-half days), but they can last indefinitely.[54]

1. **If you scored 3 or more in this category, how have you learned to identify those people with whom you are vulnerable?**

_____

_____

   What type of individuals have you been overly loyal to or most easily exploited by? List them below.

_____

_____

2. **What detachment or separation strategies might you need to develop to protect yourself from abusive people to whom you are vulnerable? (Examples might be learning to say "no", limiting phone calls or contact, staying out of chat rooms, finding new friends who don't drink, etc.)**

_____

_____

3. **What healthy relationships can you develop to replace your present toxic relationships?**

_____

_____

_____

TS ... My Score _____

Trauma Shame is prevalent among young women who have been abused and are now caught in the web of compulsive behavior. Many feel defective, worthless, and have tremendous self-hatred. After the rape, Anna saw herself as a gross and disgusting person. Guilt is a normal response, but shame goes deeper and says there is something wrong with me. Perhaps not all of me is "bad" but there is a part of me that I believe is greatly flawed or unlovable. Shame caused Anna to internalize the lies she believed.

- ❧ **Can you identify with any of these lies?[55] Say each lie out loud and circle only the ones that feel true for you:**

    I am bad and no good.

    I don't have what it takes to _____.

    I'm stupid.

    I'm worthless.

    I only have value when I'm needed.

    Whatever I do, it won't be good enough.

    My worth is based on my performance.

    If people know the real me they won't like me and they will reject me.

    I don't deserve to be happy.

    Some sins are not forgivable.

    People will love and accept me only if I'm perfect.

    I'll always fail no matter how hard I try.

    I am damaged goods.

    I have to have a boyfriend to show my value.

If you scored above three in Trauma Shame, you probably have some family of origin issues with respect to shame in your life. This can be one of the hardest things for you to identify because you have no other family with which to compare yours. Therefore, what your family did became normal for you. You will always love your family at some level; God built that into us. However, if you can't identify the origin of your shame from your family and friends, or churches, you will never get free from it.

1. **Who or what causes you to feel badly about who you are? List the sources of shame and what they target in you. (My parents tell me I am insensitive, the church leader says I'm not spiritual enough, my dad called me a slut, etc.)**

    As you can see in the example, Jessica's sources of shame were the males in her life.

Source of the shame	What the shame targets in me
Example from Jessica's life: Dad & brother	*My intelligence, creativity, femininity*

2. **Everyone has family secrets, personal secrets, or secrets in general. These secrets are toxic to our wellbeing. List some of these secrets that keep you stuck in shame.**

_____

_____

_____

3. **Identify at least two people with whom you are going to share your secrets**. If you are not certain who is a safe person for you, discuss this with your *Behind the Mask* leader or group, or with a counselor. This is a critical action step because we are only as sick as our secrets.

_____

4. **Considering the lies you circled at the beginning of the TS (Trauma Shame) section, what is the truth according to God?** List three truths about your identity and a Scripture reference for each from **"Who I am in Christ"** found in the **Resources** section in the back of this workbook. Refer to this list now and mark it as a reference page for future journaling and meditating.

A._____

B._____

C._____

TP… My Score_____

This category of **Trauma Pleasure** is huge in most who have compulsive behavior. Frequently, young women find themselves setting aside their own values and going along with some of their boyfriend's activities. Or during their childhood, the pain and shame from their own family of origin was so intense, they looked for ways to escape the pain that might have included masturbation or other sexual activities that helped mask or medicate the pain. In an attempt to anesthetize the pain and fill a sense of emptiness, it is not unusual for women who have been sexually abused to engage in many sexual relationships. Some young women also find pleasure in the power they realize they have over guys sexually. In other words, they experience the opposite of the powerlessness they had during the abuse as a child or teen.

Jessica has a friend, Melissa, who had similar trauma to Jessica. To feel as if she is giving herself worth, Melissa compulsively shops. Whenever she feels rejected, Melissa turns to online shopping or goes to the mall. When she wears new things, she feels better about herself. Her thoughts are not to reward herself because she feels valued, but rather she carries the false conception that she can add self-worth by wearing expensive clothing. Also, Melissa numbs the pain for a short time by giving herself a "high" of purchasing something expensive. After wearing it once, however, the item loses its appeal, and she must shop more to numb the pain.

Trauma Pleasure can appear differently in each of our lives. For instance, Anna escaped her pain by smoking marijuana and Cindy numbed her pain by having secret sex with her boyfriend after school. Each time, the pleasure was temporary and usually accompanied by regret or guilt.

1. **If your score was 3 or more in TP, construct a history of how excitement, danger, and/or shame have acted as an "accelerator" or "motivator" in your life.**

_____

_____

_____

2. **Now investigate the tie between excitement and shame with regards to your past trauma. Write down your insights and findings here.**

_____

_____

_____

3. **Itemize what this pleasure seeking has cost you. Listing each event or relationship and its toll on you emotionally, physically, socially, and financially.**

Event/ relationship	Emotional Costs	Physical Costs	Social Costs	Financial Costs
Example: Snuck out of the house to see my boyfriend	Betrayal to parents & my own values	Boyfriend forced me to go all the way & I am no longer a virgin	▪ He bragged about it later ▪ Loss of reputation	I was grounded for a week and lost allowance

TB ... My Score_____

Trauma Blocking as a response to pain from the past is a favorite pastime for Christian believers. TB is a pattern of numbing overwhelming feelings that are rooted in past trauma. In my own life, I realized eating certain foods (i.e. chocolate and salty snacks) was a way of numbing out when I felt overwhelmed. Procrastination was also a means of avoiding the fear of failure. At times I would try to control relationships and events when I perceived myself to be in an unsafe situation.

1. **If your score was 3 or more in TB, identify ways you have tried to numb out and avoid pain: fantasy, TV, gambling, cutting, food, control, isolation, perfectionism, procrastination, alcohol, drugs, excessive religious practices, compulsive spending, masturbation, etc.**

   _____

   _____

   _____

2. **Identify a few of those significant times of distress where you found yourself using any of these numbing behaviors to cope.**

DISTRESSFUL EVENT	COPING BEHAVIORS
Example: Rape & mom's abandonment	*Example: Cutting, lying about reality*
1.	
2.	
3.	
4.	

3. **Select one of the events you listed in the chart; describe what you were feeling and some lies you might have believed at the time** (such as fear of peer pressure, anxiety over being without a boyfriend, stress of school and grades). If you feel stuck on this, pray for the Holy Spirit to give you insight. Further help from your *Behind the Mask* group leader, a pastor, or counselor might be needed.

   _____

   _____

   _____

   _____

The material you have just worked through can be emotionally exhausting. Awareness becomes the first step to healing, and you have just taken that first step!

To seal the work you have completed, write a prayer asking God to show you, like Joseph, that what the enemy has meant for bad, God will use for His sovereign purposes.

_____

_____

_____

_____

_____

_____

_____

_____

_____

_____

Assignments

1. Read Genesis chapters 40-50.

2. Complete the next lesson.

3. Review the _"Who I Am In Christ"_ truths you selected in Chapter 6. Which 3 have been most helpful? Rewrite them here, then meditate on those truths this week.

_____

_____

_____

_____

_____

_____

_____

> **Song recommendation for meditation this week:**
> ### _Beautiful Things_
> #### _by Gungor_

Corridors of the Heart
By Angela Hutson-Cumpston

One side of the hallway is the Past, one side is the
Present, and the hallway is your Future.

Chapter 8
Grieving the Trauma

Meet Tiffany: compromising to find self-worth

I walked into the kitchen when I was about nine years old to see my stepdad groping my mom's breasts, moving his hands to her butt. "That's gross!" I said, "I don't want to see that!" My mom turned in his arms to see me standing there. "If you don't want to see it, leave the room!" my stepdad hollered. I looked at my mom. She shrugged, making a face like she wanted to leave, but couldn't help it if he were touching her that way. A lie began to form in my head: "My mom doesn't have a choice of how he touches her. I don't have a choice as to how men touch my body. It is not mine, it is theirs."

Several years later, when I was fourteen, I remember a time when my mom set me up with a 17-year-old guy to pick me up in his car. He did drugs and was definitely not someone I would pick to be my boyfriend. There was nothing safe about him, but because my mom set us up, I felt obligated to go with him on dates. She told us to have fun and waved at us as he drove me away. She knew we were going to park and make out in his car. We never had sex but we got close. I never understood why my own mom would let me go out with this guy. What kind of mom allows her daughter to go on a date with a guy like this? I liked the attention, so I dutifully waited for him by the window to pick me up so we could go make out. We broke up when my family moved a few months later, but my feelings of anger at my mom still remained. The people who were supposed to keep me safe put me in deliberate danger. Another lie began to dig into my mind: " Life is not safe. You have to please men and make them happy to be safe."

After we moved and I turned 15, I was invited to a party. Everything about this night should have sent up red flags: underage drinking, older guys, sneaking and lying to get there. I didn't see the warning signs; I only saw an innocent evening of fun with my new friends. I don't remember much about that night. I think my brain shut off a part of my memory because it was so painful. I remember becoming aware that something terrible was happening. My heart filled with fear and my body was covered in a blanket of disgust. My mind awakened to what was happening. At first I saw him. He was on top of me and I was lying exposed and naked under him. He was doing things to me that hurt and violated my body. I started the party as a virgin and ended the party no longer pure and clean. As I looked hazily around the room, unable to focus on what was happening, I saw more than one person. I closed my eyes and gave up any fight in me. Suddenly my body was not my own. They stole my virginity and took a piece of me with them. Shame, fear, and guilt replaced what they stole. Agony began to writhe deep within my heart. My body became ugly to me. I don't remember getting home that night. I don't remember who was in the room when a part of me was stolen. I don't know who knew what happened or who saw me being abused. The moment, the night, the distress, I stuffed it all into my heart. Lies that had been spoken to me made their home in my heart. My stepdad was right, I thought. I am a whore and a slut. New lies began to knit together in my thoughts. I am dirty, ugly, fearful, and disgusting.

I never told anyone what had happened to me. I didn't even know who had violated me. I didn't say anything. I detached myself from the feelings and experience and pretended that it didn't happen. I didn't want to remember the humiliation and the disgrace. I just wanted to move on. When I looked at myself in the mirror, I saw only a gross and disgusting person. I could not find peace within myself again.

―――――――――

Tiffany then coped with her pain through an eating disorder and being involved with several men. She saw herself as damaged goods. Later in her life she had two abortions and entered relationships with men who did not commit to her. Her sexuality had been taken from her when she was young and Tiffany could not reclaim it as her own until intense therapy and in-depth renewing of her brain began. She had to grieve her losses before she could move forward to establish new healthy relational patterns in her life.

In Scripture, we see that Joseph also went through major trauma in his lifetime. In Psalm 105, the writer makes some insightful observations about Joseph's life and the trauma he went through. This Psalm is a beacon of hope for every person who loves God and has gone through some very painful times in life. [56]

> *He [God] sent a man ahead of them [Jacob's family].*
> *He sent Joseph, who was sold as a slave.*
> *They hurt his feet with shackles and cut into his neck with an iron collar.*
> *The Lord's promise tested him through fiery trials until his prediction came true.*
> *The king sent someone to release him.*
> *The ruler of nations set him free.*
> *He made Joseph the master of his palace and the ruler of all his possessions.*
> *Joseph trained the king's officers the way he wanted and taught his respected leaders wisdom.*
>
> Psalm 105:17-22 (GW)

The challenge will be for you to believe that God has something far better for you than the situation you have been struggling with in your past.

Your PTSI scores may have surprised you. Often, those who are surprised begin to realize they have lived with the pain within for so long they no longer consciously recognize it. At a subconscious level the pain has never really subsided, instead they have just learned to medicate it through compulsive behavior.

The devil uses the pain of our past to try to put "iron collars" around our necks like he did with Joseph (Psalm 105:18). **But by reading the entire Psalm, we know it is just God testing His word in us, preparing us for the future authority He has set aside for each of us to step into.** That is why worshiping God helps us as we go through a pressure situation; praise declares the truth of who God is in the midst of our pain and trauma. More than ever we need to hear from God and praise Him, trusting Him for revelation and breakthrough. We have to choose not to be controlled by the fears and pain of our past, whether at a conscious or subconscious level. We serve a Lord who understands our struggles.

Hopefully you are listening to the songs that go with each chapter. The truths of these songs can begin to change the belief system and lies you have been living with. As these new truths sink in, the healing process can begin to take root.

As we walked through the PTSI evaluation and analysis, some painful struggles that you may have pushed down might have come to the surface. Looking at your specific scores is not a comfortable process. But much like Joseph, we truly begin to reign in the place uniquely set aside for us as we face our pain.

We need to place the pain within the context of God's sovereign touch on our lives.

The book of Genesis devotes nearly ten chapters to this process in Joseph's life (Genesis 40-50). For nearly 17 years (according to most scholars) he wrestled with the ongoing injustice of his situation without letting it control him. Then he is suddenly catapulted into a position of incredible prominence; it appears as if God's promise to him has finally come true.

But it is not fulfilled until Joseph faces the deep wounds of his past with his family. Repeatedly in the process Joseph is emotionally troubled to the point of tears. He was a man of unlimited power and prestige who sobbed uncontrollably as he rehearsed his childhood wounds with his brothers.

He wept aloud, and the Egyptians and the house of Pharaoh heard it.
Genesis 45:2 (NKJ)

Once Joseph's brothers realize the second in command in the most powerful nation in the world was the little brother who they attempted to kill, they are terrified. And Joseph allows the hand of God to wipe his PTSI scores clean when he declares,

"Don't be afraid. Do I act for God? Don't you see, you planned evil against me but God used those same plans for my good, as you see all around you right now—life for many people. Easy now, you have nothing to fear; I'll take care of you and your children." He reassured them, speaking with them heart-to-heart.
Genesis 50:19-21 (MSG)

Joseph's words, full of wisdom, are the doorway to your freedom from the wounds of your past. Specifically, there are **four concepts of emotional freedom from your past** that you must grasp.

#1 The trial you are going through will stop when it has accomplished God's purpose in your life. Note: this does <u>not</u> mean you need to put up with a current abuse situation; abuse is never OK; parents or counselors should be told if you are experiencing sexual or physical abuse.

Israel walked into Egypt as an extended family of 70. They hadn't even noticed that over the years they were enslaved, they had grown to millions. They had gradually turned into a nation. The traumas that your PTSI scores represent are difficulties **God did not create but will use for His purposes.** The devil can never out-maneuver God in your life or mine. Everything that has happened can be used by the hand of God *if* you let it. Only a sovereign God can pull that off, and Joseph understood that truth.

#2 Don't deny your wounds and points of betrayal.

Reading the portion of Scripture leading up to Joseph's confrontation, you see him agonizing and working through the pain inflicted upon him by his brothers. Then during the confrontation Joseph stated very clearly, "You planned evil against me." He didn't excuse their behavior or tell himself to "just ignore the pain and go on." He grieved his loss and acknowledged what had been taken from him.

As you go through your PTSI evaluation, it is important that you stop at some point and grieve. Without the grief, your actions may continue to be a response to your pain. For example, Tiffany never grieved over the abuse she faced while growing up until years later when an eating disorder almost killed her.

In this chapter we will begin grieving what was taken from you. As you face the pain, it is important to express how the wounds in your past and present make you feel and to identify what you lost in the process.

Review Tiffany's trauma chart:

My age when the trauma 1st occurred	This is what happened	Feelings & thoughts the event produced	How this affects me today
9	Saw stepdad grope mom. She didn't try to stop him & didn't help me talk about what I saw.	Confusion, scared	▪ Early loss of innocence & lack of parental boundaries. ▪ Causes me to question my own boundaries.
14	Mom encouraged me to go out with an older boy who wanted to make out.	Anger at mom; desire to be liked at any cost.	▪ I disregard my own safety in decisions I make just like my mom. ▪ I give sex to get the love I desire.
15	I was drunk & was raped by more than one guy; my virginity was stolen from me.	Fear, horror, humiliation; I felt ugly	▪ I carry a lot of shame and feel like damaged goods. ▪ Today it is hard to think of myself differently.
17	Tried to please men; unhealthy relationships with men; got an abortion.	I felt like a failure, scared	My boundaries & values are not healthy for me. Relationships end up with me being re-wounded.

~ Identify your trauma. List your age, the trauma, your feelings and thoughts, and how the trauma impacts you today. You might want to refer back to your Wounded Heart and the PTSI to complete this chart.

My Trauma Chart

My age when the trauma 1st occurred	This is what happened	Feelings & thoughts the event produced	How this affects me today

#3 Acknowledge the "trump card" of God's grace.

You can grieve and let go of the past when you realize, as Joseph did, that it is all part of God's promotional plan for you. Please notice Joseph's perspective of success. It wasn't about holding great position or power; it was about a unique ability to help others. At the bare minimum, out of your pain you have learned to empathize with other young women in your group. You also understand how it feels to take up the challenge of facing the wounds and trauma from your past while dealing with the impact of your present compulsive behaviors. God may be using all your present difficulties to raise you up in great authority to reach many other hurting young women caught in the bondage of sin and unhealthy relationship patterns. God's grace is what transforms your life from a wounded young woman to a healed warrior.

In light of the traumas you listed, think about the losses you have suffered and what you need to grieve.

Tiffany would list the following losses:
- Loss of innocence at an early age.

- Loss of parental protection.
- Loss of virginity at age 15.
- Loss of a child because of an abortion.

Joseph would have listed some of the following in his grievance story:
- Loss of safety and trust when his brothers threatened to kill him.
- Loss of his freedom when his brothers sold him into slavery.
- Loss of family and his country when he was taken to Egypt.
- Loss of his freedom again when he was put into prison because of false accusation.

ཀ **List the losses you will need to grieve because of what has happened to you.**

_____

_____

_____

_____

_____

_____

_____

_____

_____

ཀ **Now incorporate the work you have done in this chapter into a story. Make sure you write it in third person using "she" and "her" pronouns. This will help you step back and look at what you experienced from the perspective of an objective observer. In other words, you want to try to see how others would look at your life and your story.**

Once upon a time there was a little girl ....

_____

_____

_____

_____

_____

_____

_____

_____

_____

_____

_____

_____

_____

_____

_____

_____

_____

_____

_____

_____

_____

_____

_____

_____

_____

_____

_____

#4 Learn to live "heart-to-heart."

Think again about the Genesis story of Joseph where he sobbed uncontrollably as he rehearsed his childhood wounds with his brothers. When we grieve those losses, God releases something new in us. We see a graciousness released in Joseph toward the very people who betrayed him in Genesis 50:21, **"He assured them, speaking with them heart-to-heart."** He didn't speak "to them" but "with them." Because of our shame, the tendency is to attack others or isolate and avoid intimacy. Joseph did none of these.

You sharing your story will help you break isolation and allow others to grieve with you over the losses you have experienced. Your heart-to-heart sharing begins to move you out of the isolation that previously led to compulsive behavior.

❧ **Write a prayer asking God to begin this process of grieving heart-to-heart with Him and others.**

_____

_____

_____

_____

_____

_____

_____

_____

_____

_____

Song recommendation for meditation this week:
Forever and a Day
by Bethel Live

Chapter 9
Exposing Lies that Lie Behind the Mask

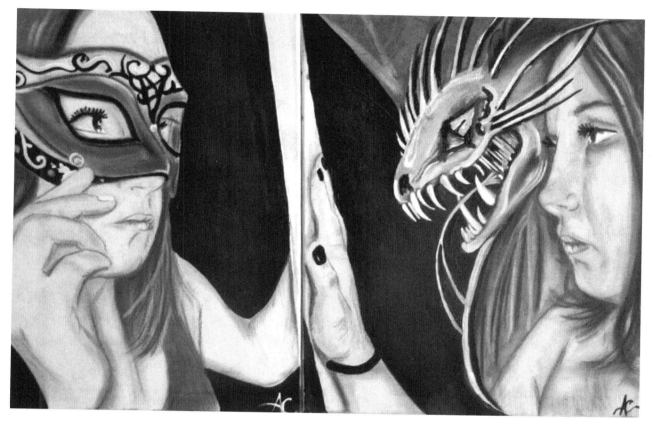

"Facing the Truth"

The masks we wear have become a way of hiding the shame we feel about who we are. Remember, **guilt** says: "I did something wrong," but **shame** says: "There is something wrong with me." Shame and the lies we believe about who we are drive our unhealthy compulsive behavior. These lies are lodged deep in our subconscious brain, deposited by the enemy. We believe these lies and securely fastened the mask so no one will know who we believe we are. In this lesson we want to look deep under the trauma and wounds and discover the lies we have believed and tried to hide.

It takes **courage** to admit you are not perfect. It takes **compassion** toward yourself as you are uncovering the shame to discover the source of the lies. It takes **connecting** with your group members to risk being vulnerable and acknowledging the truth. For you to have worked through eight chapters, it is evident you are up to the challenge.

Where did these lies come from?

Because the prefrontal cortex is not fully developed until the mid-twenties, your brain is limited in logically thinking through the trauma you have experienced. You interpret your experiences through a child's understanding. And guess what, the enemy wants to help you put the worst spin possible on your beliefs about those events in your life and about who you are. He does not want you to believe the truth: that you are worthy of love and connection for no other reason than being a unique creation and the apple of God's eye.

Even in a perfect world the enemy is at work causing us to question God and ourselves. It was a perfect world (without sin) in the Garden of Eden where Satan said to the woman:

> *"...you will not surely die. For God knows that the day you eat of it your eyes will be opened and you will be like God, knowing good and evil."*
> Genesis 3:4-5 (NKJ)

The enemy's lies in this statement include the following:

- What God has said is not true (you won't die).
- God is withholding something good from you.
- You can't trust God to know what is best for you.
- You can become like God yourself.

To discover the lies we subconsciously believe, let's first review what we learned about trauma by looking at it from a little different perspective. Essentially trauma can impact us in two ways:

1. Through **acts of commission** which are those things done to us such as abuse, betrayal, loss, or abandonment.

2. Through **acts of omission** which are those things that were not given to us, such as unconditional love, provision, safety, and a sense of attachment.

We have looked at testimonies of three women who have experienced trauma. Let's see how acts of commission and omission have played out in their lives.

Anna : Love at any Cost

Anna learned to avoid pain by giving in to demands of others. You heard part of her story in previous chapters. As you read more of her testimony, be prepared to identify and distinguish between the acts of commission and omission.

In seventh grade, I confided in my boyfriend that I had been raped by my mom's boyfriend, repeatedly, from ages 11 to 13. I was testing to see if I could ever be loved in spite of what had happened to me. I lost that bet. The next day, everyone at school had heard my deepest secret, that I had been raped. I felt like damaged goods and unworthy of love. Knowing that people I didn't even know knew my dark secret filled me with so much shame! The shame crushed me. I couldn't run from the memories that lived in my body. What had happened to me was now defining me. Again, a person whom I was supposed to have trusted had betrayed me.

Anna broke up with her boyfriend and then struggled making connections with healthy friends during sixth and seventh grade. By her eighth grade year, she escaped the shame by transferring to a school in a different town where no one knew her. That year, while visiting her cousin, Anna met and was pursued by 18-year-old Clark. He eventually asked her to send nude pictures of herself. She did. He continued to text her sexual messages and pressured her to move beyond the boundaries she had set for herself. Anna refused his advances and tried to break it off with him. However, Clark did not take "no" for an answer. He started stalking her through texting and his words got more and more aggressive. She told him to leave her alone.

Furious that he was being rejected by such a young girl, Clark created a Myspace profile using Anna's name and posted her nude pictures next to other vulgar pictures taken from porn sites. Imagine the shame that Anna must have felt! To make matters worse, Clark invited everyone on her current friends list to add her nude profile to their Myspace profiles. Guess who was on her current friends lists? All of her new friends from her new school. She was mortified.

Anna walked through the halls at school the next few weeks dodging strange looks from dozens of middle school boys and the whispers of girls who had access to her pornographic profile. They all now had literally seen her naked and exposed. Anna was referred to the school counselor, and charges were pressed against the young man. It took a month and a half for Myspace to remove the false profile. Legal proceedings went on for months, but her reputation in that school was ruined. She transferred schools again, trying to find a safe place where others might not have heard of her story.

✎ **What acts of trauma commission did Anna experience?**

_____

_____

_____

✎ **What acts of trauma omission did she experience?**

_____

_____

_____

The Noose of Addiction[57]

> **Addictive Root**
> - Family dysfunction
> - Personal trauma
> - Addictive society

> **Addictive Mindset**
> Destructive Core Concepts:
> - Worthless
> - Unlovable
> - Alone
> - Sexual High

In looking at the Addictive Root, we see how the trauma Anna experienced as a child and middle school student opened the door to an Addictive Mindset of feeling unlovable, abandoned, and lonely. Her feelings of love and acceptance came when she realized she could be loved and needed if she gave men sex or exposed her body to them. She sought comfort from men to heal the wounds of her childhood, hoping to feel normal.

Lies and core beliefs that have controlled Anna and other young women include:

____ I am not in control of my own body.
____ I am alone and no one can or will protect me.
____ I am only good for one thing—sex.
____ To be loved, I have to please others even at the expense of my own safety and well-being.
____ I can control guys with sex.
____ Having power over guys gives me value.
____ If I can control my relationships I will be safe.
____ If I have a guy in my life, I have value.
____ I can't be alone.
____ I am loved if I have a guy in my life.
____ I am complete if I have a guy in my life.
____ I am not allowed to be sad, angry, or unhappy.

👌 **Check the above statements that might be part of your core beliefs.**

Most young women with compulsive sexual behavior are under the false impression that if they have power over men, they can get their way and feel safe. The truth is, when this unhealthy approach is taken they are creating unsustainable relationships. This illusion of power helps them avoid facing their own fears, doubts and insecurities.

Cindy: validation through sex

Cindy learned to avoid pain by using sex to cope. As you read her testimony, be prepared to identify and distinguish between the acts of commission and omission.

My dad left our family when I was 18 months old and my parents divorced soon after. The man who was supposed to take care of me and be there for me was absent. My mom raised me, but I still knew my dad somewhat, even though he lived in another town.

Then, when I was 10 years old, my dad committed suicide. For 18 years, people around me told me that I should "just get over it." It hurt to see other daughters with their dads, knowing that I would never experience that kind of love. I wanted to believe that God loved me, but the only dad I knew was the one who was absent, the one who had left me and then had taken his own life. I felt like I was not worth being around if he would rather kill himself than stay on earth to be with me. I have lived my whole life just wanting to be held by my daddy and will never be able to experience that on this earth.

After Luke and I started having sex our junior year, I felt like I could not live without him. My senior year I got a half-ride scholarship to a really great private Christian college and had a decision to make. There was this incredible opportunity in front of me. I could be immersed in a Christian community and get an education in something I really wanted to do. It was a few states away though, and Luke was not going to be able to follow me out there. When trying to decide what to do, I did not feel confident leaving my boyfriend to follow my dreams. So, I stayed in my little hometown. Instead of going to college I worked at the local bank. We got married a few years later. Three months into our marriage, I found out he was using pornography. I felt used, lonely, and betrayed. We started working opposite schedules and rarely saw each other during the days.

At work I was finding great success and affirmation. Then one day a man came into work and caught my attention. I never knew I could have such a raw sexual connection and craving for someone, much less someone who was not my husband. We began talking and I began flirting. He was handsome and affirmed and appreciated who I was. In my head, I expected this man to be everything I wished my husband was not. I fantasized about a relationship with this prince charming who would rescue me from my unhappiness. It wasn't long before we hooked up, even though it was something I never thought I would do. I couldn't live the double life and finally confessed to my husband. We separated and I broke up with the man at work.

☙ **What acts of trauma <u>commission</u> did Cindy experience?**

_____

_____

☙ **What acts of trauma <u>omission</u> did she experience?**

_____

_____

In an effort to fill the void Cindy's dad left, we see TR (Trauma Repetition) and TBD (Trauma Bonding) taking place in her life. She is repeating unhealthy choices to try to find that belonging and connectedness she missed as a child. She was willing to sacrifice a great education and now a marriage to medicate pain that goes all the way back to age 10.

Lies and core beliefs:

_____ I must have a man in my life to feel secure.
_____ I feel loved and valued if I have a guy in my life.
_____ I can't be alone; I am complete with a guy in my life.
_____ Prince Charming will rescue me.
_____ I can't be happy without _____ (friends, drugs, parties, a boyfriend, etc.) in my life.
_____ I might marry the wrong guy.
_____ I only feel valued when I am with him.

☙ **Check the statements that might be part of your core beliefs.**

Women like Cindy who struggle with love and romance addiction have allowed the obsession of fantasy to rule a lot of their mind time. The "what ifs" and the secret desires add to the high they experience.

Both Anna and Cindy had elements of codependency (unhealthy dependency on relationships) mixed in with their compulsive love/sexual behavior. They both to some extent needed to be needed by a man and felt dependent on a man to be valued. But Jessica found herself trapped in love addiction out of a codependent need to please and be valued. Look for the acts of trauma commission and omission she experienced.

Jessica: pleasing for love

Jessica learned to avoid pain by pleasing others. As you read her testimony, be prepared to identify and distinguish between the acts of commission and omission

Jessica lived on a tightrope. She had grown up in the church and regularly attended youth group. She knew that she was supposed to feel loved, but unconditional love was foreign to her. The love within her family dangled on strings. She believed the lie that she had to be good and do the right things in order to deserve love from her parents. As Jessica went through puberty, the regular stream of criticism, sarcasm, and teasing in her home environment affected her mind, like needles poking her skin thousands of times. Jessica tried to avoid this pain by changing herself to please others.

When her friends got their ears pierced in fourth grade, her parents prevented her from doing so. After this experience, she felt that her parents and God would not love her as much if she got her ears pierced. When Jessica got her period, her brother made fun of her so she hid her femininity from him so that he would accept her. When Jessica tried to emulate other girls or women with appearance or by forming relationships with guys, she felt criticized, her feelings minimized.

In high school, when a guy asked her out after a tennis match that ended at 8:30, her dad made 9 o'clock her curfew. Jessica obeyed. Even though her dad just wanted to keep her safe, his control in her life made Jessica feel incapable of taking care of herself as a woman. The relationship with the guy never amounted to anything and Jessica grew bitter at her dad for his strict rules. She had many rules in her life, but not a relationship with her parents built on mutual respect or trust. The shame kept her from breaking the rules, and her loyalty to her family kept her from saying anything to change it. Jessica turned to fantasy relationships to ease her pain created from the tension in her home. Jessica also learned that she was unable to live without a man, her dad in this case, to make decisions for her.

ᔰ **What acts of trauma <u>commission</u> did Jessica experience?**

_____

_____

ᔰ **What acts of trauma <u>omission</u> did she experience?**

_____

_____

Although Jessica was raised in a loving home, there were huge expectations put on her to perform. Anything short of that would displease her parents. She had to put aside her desires and safety to protect the image she felt she needed to maintain. The following are some of Jessica's core beliefs.

Core beliefs:

    ____ I have to do everything perfect to be OK.
    ____ I should never make mistakes.
    ____ I owe others because I have been given so much.
    ____ Our family must appear perfect and it is up to me to make it happen.
    ____ My needs are not important.
    ____ If I please him, I'm a good person.
    ____ I will do anything for a loving relationship.
    ____ My value comes from what I can do for others.

✎ **Check the statements that might be part of your core beliefs.**

Monica and Abby: Same-sex attraction

Monica is now a young adult who struggles with same-sex attraction. She, like many adolescents, has responded out of peer pressure and her own trauma. Raised in a family with lots of rules and very little relationship, like Jessica, she was starved for close emotional connection. Her parents were very strict about her seeing boys, so she and her best girlfriend Abby began exploring each other sexually. Sadly, Abby, who initiated this exploration, had been sexually abused by her dad and raped by a boy she dated from church. Both were trying to meet legitimate needs of closeness and connectedness in a way that would later affect their brain maps. New pathways were being formed in their brains as they tried to medicate their pain by seeking unnatural ways to soothe that pain.

Here are some of the lies and beliefs that were driving their behaviors:

Monica
    ____ Any relationship is better than no relationship.
    ____ I am enjoying the friendship and sex; how could it be wrong?
    ____ Since I can't date boys yet, this is a good substitute.
    ____ Other girls are doing it.
    ____ We are just experimenting.

Abby
    ____ Men will hurt you if you get close to them.
    ____ Men can't be trusted.
    ____ Women are safe and won't hurt you like men do.

Sadly, neither of these young women understood two facts:

1. During adolescence the brain is making huge changes and is creating pathways of thinking that will follow them into adulthood. Statistics tell us that 55% of young women by the time they reach age 18 will have viewed same-sex porn.[58] Habitually viewing this kind of porn will change your brain. Some, like Abby, struggle with same-sex desires because they have found boys to be unsafe. They turn to girlfriends to meet their emotional and sexual needs.

Also, young women's bodies are beautiful to look at compared to boy's bodies. In the creation chapters of Genesis, Scripture says God created Adam out of dust and He uses only one verse to describe Adam's creation. In creating Eve, six verses are used and they imply she was fashioned, sculpted, and a picture of beauty. God designed her to be attractive and to become one with Adam.

2. The enemy would like to captivate and confuse young women with same-sex attraction. When exposed to porn images, especially in the teen years, unhealthy imaginations develop and deepen the brain pathways that cause Christian adolescents to violate Scripture and bring them into bondage. Scripture warns that sexual activity outside of marriage not only damages and destroys the marriage relationship, but also will cause us to forfeit our ability to inherit the kingdom of God.

> *Do you not know that the unrighteous will not inherit the kingdom of God? Do not be deceived. Neither fornicators, nor idolaters, nor adulterers, nor homosexuals, nor sodomites.....will inherit the kingdom of God.*
> 1 Corinthians 6: 9-10 (NKJ)

It is true God loves us unconditionally. However, when we choose these activities we are removing ourselves from His presence. It reminds me of a bumper sticker I once saw, "If God seems far away, guess who moved?"

If you, like many young women, are struggling with these issues there is some good news. Proverbs 4 declares that if you are willing to guard your heart and walk the righteous road of wisdom, blessings will be a part of your life: *Above all and before all, do this: Get wisdom!* (implying God's ways will bring you that wisdom) Proverbs 4:5 (MSG)

> *Cherish wisdom. It will raise you up. It will bring you honor when you embrace it. It will give you a graceful garland for your head. It will hand you a beautiful crown.*
> Proverbs 4:8-9 (GW-God's Word)

When you begin to identify the lies and understand the trauma or pain that is driving these false beliefs, Scripture says every thought can be taken captive:

> *Casting down imaginations, and every high thing that exalteth itself against the knowledge of God, and bringing into captivity every thought to the obedience of Christ....*
> 2 Corinthians 10:5 (KJV)

After recognizing, spiritually renouncing, and pulling down these false imaginations, new healthy experiences will help reprogram your brain. As you develop healthy emotional connectedness with young women in your *Behind the Mask* group, these memorable experiences can literally restructure your brain.[59]

The trauma of Cindy's life led her to go down the path of finding validation through sex. The trauma of Anna's life caused her to go down the path of love/romance addiction. Jessica's trauma thrust her into codependent behavior; she worked hard to project the illusion and image that she could handle anything. Monica's desire for closeness threw her into an unhealthy same-sex relationship and Abby's abuse from males caused her to seek out closeness through unhealthy female companionship.

❧ With which of these women can you most identify? (It may be a combination of two or more). Explain your response.

_____

_____

_____

_____

❧ Look back at your trauma story and write down the acts of commission you experienced.

_____

_____

_____

_____

❧ Write down the acts of omission you experienced.

_____

_____

_____

❧ Now look back over your Wounded Heart diagram in Chapter 6; list each trauma (past & present hurts) and the lie or core belief that emerged from what you experienced.

Past & Present Hurts (transfer your responses from your Wounded Heart)	Lie or Core Belief
Example: My parents divorced	People I love will abandon me

You cannot change your hurts and trauma; that is part of your history. But you can identify lies attached to the history that drive you to continue in compulsive and unhealthy behavior.

As a young adult, your prefrontal cortex is still being developed. As I went back through my own history and the trauma's and lies I experienced, I observed an interesting phenomena. I was immediately amazed at the fact that after age 21, I could not think of any new lies. The lies that were connected to later traumas were only repeats of the old lies that were core beliefs before age 21. All the lies beyond age 21 were a little more sophisticated versions of the old lies.

How could this be? The Holy Spirit took me back to the information we discovered about the pre-frontal cortex (the logic center in our brain) that was not fully developed.

Now, put the information about the brain with the Scripture in 1 Corinthians that states:

> **When I was a child, I talked like a child, I thought like a child, I reasoned like a child. When I became a man (woman), I put childish ways behind me.**
> 1 Corinthians 13: 11 (NIV)

In other words, as a grown adult, I need to put childish thinking away. Now let's put this information together. I realized that when I went through trauma as a child, the enemy was immediately present to interpret events and put his spin on my reality. Once I became a solid Christian at the age of 21, I was able to reason clearly and I could put away new lies. But the old lies had great power over me because they had been established from childhood and I hadn't fully identified them as lies.

Most of us are unaware of those lies and core beliefs that travel through our brains on a daily basis. Remember, the lies and your response to them can keep you stuck in your compulsive behavior and cause you to continue wearing a mask to hide the shame of the lies you believe. Once you identify the lies, they need to be replaced with truth.

Think back over the young women's stories in this chapter. It is important to note that they were vulnerable not just from the trauma they experienced, but also because of the lies that were attached to those traumas. Let's review one lie that was embedded in each of their traumas and counter it with the truth.

- The absence of a father and abandonment she endured as a child caused Cindy to let men decide her value. She used sex to gain value and validation.

Cindy's lie: *I cannot be happy or valued without a man in my life.*
Cindy's truth: ***In Christ I never have to feel abandoned; He said he would never leave me.***

- Surviving intense sexual abuse led Anna to find love by sacrificing her body to give pleasure to men.

Anna's lie: *If others get their sexual needs met, then I have value and will be loved.*
Anna's truth: ***I can't control anyone but myself. I can stay safe by setting healthy boundaries and learning to say no.***

- The emotional absence from her father and growing up in a rigid home environment led Jessica to give up her own identity and her own needs to keep a good image and please everyone else.

<u>Jessica's lie</u>: *My value comes from meeting the needs of others and making everything look good.*
<u>Jessica's truth</u>: **I am accepted by Jesus, not for what I can do, but because of what Christ has done for me.**

- Monica's lack of authentic closeness within her family of origin threw her into an unhealthy same-sex relationship.

<u>Monica's lie</u>: *Intimacy and closeness can only come from other girls.*
<u>Monica's truth</u>: **God designed me to be intimate with the opposite sex and He will give me the closeness I need in healthy ways.**

- Abby's abuse from males caused her to seek closeness through unhealthy female companionship.

<u>Abby's lie</u>: *Safety can only be found in females. Guys will always hurt you.*
<u>Abby's truth</u>: **Safety can be found in Christ. He can lead me to healthy male relationships.**

How can you discover the truth?
You may want to spend time before the Lord asking Him for new pictures of how He sees you and then attach a Scripture from the ones listed in "Who I Am In Christ" in the *Resources* section of this book.

The following exercise can help you.

- **Pick one of the lies and ask Jesus to show you the truth and give you a new picture about that truth to replace the lie you have believed.**

Example: One woman I counseled admitted not feeling loved because of some of the trauma she had experienced in her past. She said she felt like a rock and that water (love) flowing over her was always intended for someone else. God gave her a new picture—that He made her to be a sponge and that as water (love) came her way, He had created her to absorb the water (love). When the sponge was full, the water would flow through her to others and bless them.

Example: Another young woman had horrible words spoken over her by her stepdad that labeled her as stupid. The old picture she had was one of the word "Stupid" made out of stone and placed over her head for all to see. In her new picture, she saw God's gigantic hand crushing the stone into sand and replacing it with His banner of love over her.

Spend some time listening to Jesus. Draw a picture of a lie you have believed about yourself in the past. Then draw a new picture that reflects what God says about you.

Old picture that is a lie	New truth picture from God

🙢 Now transfer all the lies from your Past & Present Hurts chart. Place the truth (God's truth) next to each lie.

Lie or Core Belief from the Hurt

Lie or core belief from the hurt	God's Truth about me
Example: I will always be abandoned by those closest to me.	He showed me He would not leave me (Hebrews 13:5—He will not desert me nor forsake me.)

❧ In the future, spend time drawing pictures of the new truths God wants to impart in your life and meditate on them daily.

Song recommendation for meditation this week:
True Things
by JJ Heller

Assignment: Read the next chapter and complete the exercises.

"The Struggle"

Purity is about beauty, street smarts, and power. When a bride is pure, she wields a powerful weapon.

-Angela-

Chapter 10
The Facade of Fantasy

Recently we (Diane with husband Ted) were watching one of our granddaughters dance in the family room. She was doing a beautiful ballet routine that was enchanting. Ted asked her, "Are you a ballerina?" She looked at him as if grandpa didn't have a clue and said, "I am a prima ballerina!" The fantasies of children are awesome.[60]

We all have fantasies. What are your fantasies in life? Have you pictured yourself as having the career of your dreams, finding the perfect soul mate, being the perfect wife?

❧ **List several fantasies you have had about romance, dating, marriage, and living happily ever after:**

1. _____
2. _____
3. _____
4. _____

❧ **List fantasies you have about what the perfect family would look like:**

1. _____
2. _____
3. _____
4. _____

❧ **Maybe you have fantasies focused on achievement such as education, sports, a career, and or using your gifts or talents before thousands. What are your achievement fantasies?**

1. _____
2. _____
3. _____
4. _____

Where are we headed with this? The fantasies in your life can give you an intriguing window into your soul. It is usually when you are under pressure that some of your deepest fantasies can surface. God gave us the ability to dream and imagine and fantasize so that we will be challenged to reach farther than we might think is humanly possible.

Therefore: God-inspired fantasy can be healing.

On the flip side, one of the most harmful and deadly aspects of love/sexual compulsive behavior is getting caught up in the cycle and facade of fantasy. This type of fantasy includes obsession and preoccupation with mental images of romance and/or pornography. Fantasy can become an unconscious strategy to escape the lonely, painful reality of present circumstances and a means of escaping true intimacy. Fantasy can sexualize the environment, supercharge relationships and frequently involves compulsive masturbation. Anxiety and/or depression usually drive the need for this type of escape.

Therefore: Fantasy used to medicate pain can be destructive.

Scripture gives us a perfect example of how fantasy can become a means of trying to escape our present reality. When pressure started mounting for the people of Israel who had left Egypt and a life of slavery, we see unreasonable thinking and fantasy beginning to flow from their minds and lips:

> *In the desert the whole community grumbled against Moses and Aaron. The Israelites said to them, "If only we had died by the Lord's hand in Egypt! There we sat around pots of meat and ate all the food we wanted, but you have brought us out into this desert to starve this entire assembly to death."*
> *Exodus 16: 2-3 (NIV)*

You'd think with all this whining they sat around in Egypt having fondue with the Pharaoh! In reality they were working night and day as slaves, getting their backs ripped open by the whips of vicious taskmasters. How could their thoughts have been so distorted?

An even deeper question: How do we deal with the distorted thinking that lies at the root of our love addiction and sexual issues? At the foundation of all compulsive behavior will be cognitive distortions, also known as garbled thinking.

↪ **Think of a time when your mind turned to fantasy.** Examples: through TV, movies, romance novels, daydreaming, etc.

What were you escaping from? What benefit did you receive from moving into times of fantasy?

_____

_____

_____

_____

The Apostle Paul challenges us in the New Testament to take every thought captive and not allow our imaginations to run wild: *We demolish arguments and every pretension that sets itself up against the knowledge of God, and we take captive every thought to make it obedient to Christ.* (2 Corinthians 10:5-NIV) So what does that mean? In today's world there are a number of self-help options touted as being the solution:

"The three-second rule" - You are told that if you have a destructive fantasy, you have three seconds to get rid of "IT." There is one huge problem; that approach doesn't work for the simple reason that the more you try to get rid of the fantasy, the more you think about "IT." Also, recent discoveries in neuroscience reveal you don't have three seconds; instead you have about three tenths of a second to get rid of "IT." So the trick is not to think of "IT" in the first place.

"The rubber band approach" - Some Christian speakers recommend this approach. You are supposed to snap the rubber band on your wrist every time you have a negative fantasy. This is a behavioral conditioning approach. Guess what? You are not like Pavlov's dog. This approach has been tried in sex offender programs and it clearly doesn't work. The cattle prod approach will never bring you to real freedom.

So, what does work? For starters, realize your thoughts are not your enemy. The enemy is the enemy. Your thoughts can be messengers of the deepest longings of your soul. Once you understand the messenger and the message concerning your longings, then the stage is set for real healing to begin.

Fantasies usually reveal desires or deep longings in three areas.

1. **Some fantasies replay a past event expecting, or at least hoping for, a different outcome.**

   Examples:
   - A young woman might replay an abusive situation in her mind and try to figure out what she did to cause the abuse; in reality, she was a victim with no power to change the outcome.
   - Someone jilted by a boyfriend might keep replaying what she could have done differently to save the relationship.

2. **Other fantasies are desires that have never been fulfilled.**

   Examples:
   - Having a musical gift, but passed over for the part for which she auditioned.
   - Not making the cheer leading team.
   - Not having a dad figure in her life.

3. **The fantasy repeats an event that happened early in the individual's life that was nurturing.**

   Examples:
   - Had a male best friend at an early age and became clingy with male relationships, trying to again find that nurturing relationship.
   - Keeps looking for a family like her grandparents, as they were safe and parents were not safe.
   - Moved and lost close friends; to fill the void, she accepts anyone who will be a friend.

❧ **To which of these three fantasy categories can you relate? Give an example.**

_____

_____

_____

_____

_____

Looking into the mirror of your fantasy...

I don't recommend the Harry Potter series for general reading because of the heavy demonic tone at times. But there is one scene in *The Sorcerer's Stone*[61] that presents the power of fantasy with gripping insight. It deals with the Mirror of Esired. The dean of Hogwarts (the school Harry attends) learns that Harry and a friend have been staring into the mirror; he warns the boys of the disastrous potential of such an act. He tells them the power of the mirror is that it reflects your deepest desires. For Harry, it was gazing on his murdered parents, with them looking back on him with approval and affirmation. Harry's friend looked in the mirror and saw himself as successful and out from under the shadow of his brothers. The dean's warning to the two boys carried a unique insight into our deepest addictions. He tells them people have literally been captured by the mirror and are unable to leave. The name Erised is "Desire" spelled backwards!

The dean's point is that fantasy is a way to avoid the reality of our situation. Harry is never going to bring his parents back. Instead, he needs to grieve the loss and find his affirmation from another source in the present. Harry's friend is better served by creating his own place of significance rather than living in a fantasy.

Maturity and healing take place in our lives when we pursue reality at all costs. The mirror of Erised[62] in today's world has frequently been found through Internet pornography or chat rooms. With a simple click of the mouse you can enter a dream world where every fantasy is fulfilled by a willing and ever-ready man or image. Such potential hook-ups and images constantly promise to meet our deepest romantic and sexual cravings.

Fantasies are actually mirrors of our deepest wounds, hurts and disappointments in life. The mirror of Erised can become a powerful tool for our healing if we don't let it pull us in. Instead, we need to look in the mirror of our deepest romantic/sexual desires with total honesty by the grace of God.

What is your romantic/sexual desire?

We all have them and just because you have said "Yes" to Christ doesn't mean that God drained all the hormones out of your body. Christians have romantic fantasies. They only become dangerous and damaging when we don't acknowledge them.

❧ **List your ideal romantic fantasies. These are the ones that can easily have a real grip on your life. What are the romantic pictures in your mirror of Erised?**

Examples: Jessica might write, "I dream of romantically dating and maybe hooking up with my close guy friend even though we have never even talked about dating." Cindy would say, "I fantasize over the rich, easy, safe, and secure future I will have if I sleep with the millionaire at work."

1 _____

2 _____

3 _____

4 _____

Now review your responses about romance, dating, family and achievements at the beginning of this chapter. Compare them to your romantic fantasies.

> **What are some common patterns you see in all these lists?** Seeing the patterns will help you begin to uncover the reason you have struggled so deeply with romantic/sexual issues in your life.

Examples: Jessica would write, "I wanted to be desired as a woman and feel safe around men." Cindy would say, "I want to feel significant but really feel insecure. I hooked up with someone who was rich to make me feel secure but he still abandoned and betrayed me."

1 _____
2 _____
3 _____
4 _____

As you look at the patterns, what does all this tell you about your deepest desires? Where do they come from? Possibly it is something very painful that occurred early in your life, like Harry Potter's friend who was always demeaned by his older brother.

Think back over your trauma test and story and see if there is something in your past that demeaned or devalued you that you might subconsciously be trying to resolve. Or maybe it is a truth about yourself that you have been avoiding.

> **Behind our deep desires usually lies a wound that has yet to be touched by the grace of God. What are those wounds for you?**

Examples: Jessica would write, "My family's criticism has made my home an unsafe place emotionally, and I feel threatened by men. Dreaming of a relationship that isn't really there creates a place I can go mentally and feel those needs are being met."

Cindy might say, "I was wounded deeply by my dad leaving me and my husband choosing other women over me. Dating a millionaire gives me a chance to fantasize that I won't have to experience that pain again. I felt good about myself that he would even choose me."

The sources of my "Erised":

1 _____
2 _____
3 _____
4 _____

For this portion of the lesson it is critical that you share your responses with the entire group. Yes, it is going to be tough but at some point you need to realize you can't get healed on your own or by trying harder.

∾ **Pause for a moment and think of the cost of not fully acknowledging these wounds so far in your life. Then write a prayer expressing to God what you have discovered and how difficult it might be to acknowledge this to others.**

Dear God,

_____

_____

_____

_____

_____

_____

_____

_____

_____

Song recommendation for meditation this week:
American Dream
by Switchfoot

Assignment: Read the next chapter and complete the exercises.

Chapter 11
Breaking Out of Crazy Patterns

Cindy writes:

I was the one who always pushed for more commitment from my boyfriend Luke. I had given up my virginity for him and gave him my entire body to feel close to him. What I got in return was not enough. He seemed satisfied but after the initial high, sex left me feeling empty. I knew it was wrong, so I hid it from my solid Christian family, terrified they would find out. I thought I would feel better if I married him, hoped that it would take some of the guilt away. I also thought it would help make me complete and diminish the pain in my heart. At the time, I was not confiding with older trustworthy women about my insecurities or working through them in counseling. I was alone, buried under the covers of shame.

We got married fairly young. We had our good moments, but issues in our relationship did not diminish; instead, they magnified. We worked opposite schedules and grew apart. He was coping with his issues in unhealthy ways and I felt I couldn't help myself from also seeking affirmation elsewhere. A decades-old wound caused by my absent father kept nagging me and was not healed by marrying my boyfriend. This marriage was not what I had signed up for.

I started seeing a male coworker who paid attention to me. My head filled with the fantasy of how I would be treated if I were with him instead of my husband. One thing led to the next, and I soon found him in my bed.

Shame filled me, but I pushed it down. I valued the temporary relief this fantasy relationship gave me more than I valued myself. I felt trapped in my marriage and trapped by the shame of what I had done. Lies filled my head about who I was and what I stood for. Believing the lies and keeping them hidden catapulted me into a destructive cycle. Real intimacy scared the heck out of me. My secret relationship temporarily eased the pain, but in reality it only made the situation worse.

I hid my infidelity well. My best friends and family had no idea. Despite my attempts to hide my sin, my husband discovered what I had been doing. The night he found out all hell broke loose. He threw picture frames, chairs, anything he could get his hands on. But worse than that, he shoved the phone in my face and demanded that I call my Christian mom and stepdad and confess to them what I had done. I was mortified. A 20-year-old fear of abandonment and rejection pounded in my heart. Humiliation poured over me. The lies I had believed and the voices I had followed resonated in my ears and I could hear nothing else.

I called my mom and confessed through tears. She and my stepdad immediately came over even though it was three in the morning after Luke had stormed out. What happened next blew apart the lies in my head. What my mother's love did in my darkest moment of shame calmed my fears of rejection. The grace with which my stepdad reacted made room for truth to pour in. I started to understand God's truth about me rather than the lies I had believed for so long. Maybe there was hope for me after all.

While my step-dad took a broom and cleaned up the broken glass and debris from our argument, my mother crawled into bed with me. She held me tight and let me cry in her arms. The one place from which I had been hiding for fear of rejection was a source of healing for me that night.

I know there are so many ways my parents could have reacted to me and what I had done. I am forever grateful that my parents showed me Jesus that night. My heart was stretched as my mom introduced me to a new concept I had never let myself experience before: grace.

———

For centuries, Jesus has extended His healing grace to those who are ashamed. Where others focus first on correction and condemnation, Jesus offers grace to the hurting. In John 8, a woman like Cindy had been caught in adultery. The Pharisees dragged her to Jesus to figure out what to do with her. Moses' Old Testament Law said such a woman should be stoned. After asking Jesus what to do with the woman, He responded, *"If any one of you is without sin, let him be the first to throw a stone at her."* John 8:7 (NIV)

Each man dropped his stone of accusation. The woman's life was saved! Jesus, the only man without sin who could have condemned her, asked, *"Where are your accusers?"* She commented that there were none. It was then Jesus made a life-changing comment, ***"Then neither do I condemn you. Go and sin no more."*** He spoke correction to her without a hint of condemnation.

Christ gave her the gift of no condemnation SO THAT she could sin no more.[63]

With that gift of grace, this woman and Cindy were faced with a new choice. Jesus explains that new choice to the disciples:

> ***Then Jesus said to the disciples, "If any of you wants to be my follower, you must put aside your selfish ambitions, shoulder your cross, and follow me. If you try to keep your life for yourself, you will lose it. But if you give up your life for me, you will find true life."***
> Matthew 16:24-25 (NLT)

To find this new life, Jesus often asks us to give up our old life and old patterns. This risky choice can be painful. Putting aside self-focus is hard. Daily sacrificing the familiar life and trusting God to give us true life will be difficult.

When Cindy, like the woman caught in adultery, chose to step out of her patterns of using sex for validation, she felt vulnerable and fearful of emotional intimacy. It was painful for her to resist her urge to satisfy her sexual desires and trust that God had a new life for her that would fill her deep heart wounds.

Throughout the previous chapters, we have identified our denial, trauma, and preventative measures to avoid going back into behavior that substitutes intensity for intimacy. For instance, tracking on the FASTER scale is a daily check as to where our mind and heart are. When we do this, we take back the territory that the enemy (Satan) has stolen from us. The lies that were embedded into our thought patterns at a young age are deflated of their power as we live out the truth God has revealed to us.

This chapter will give you tools to become proactive in taking back territory the enemy has taken away. It is important for you to meditate on Matthew 16:24-25, as you will gain insight into how to take back territory that was stolen. Jesus is helping you to see that the moment you deny yourself of selfish desires you have removed yourself from the realm of the enemy's control.

What areas of your life runs counter to God's best for you? What would you find hard to give up, even if you knew God's best does not include that behavior?

Examples:
- An unhealthy relationship
- Gossip
- Out-of-control sexual behavior with my boyfriend
- My tendency to isolate
- Texting or social networking when I should be doing homework

&. **Write a prayer asking God to help you identify those areas of your life that run counter to His best.**

_____

_____

_____

_____

_____

_____

Notice Jesus doesn't say, "Take my cross," but rather, "Take up your cross." His cross was to die for the sins of the world; that is obviously not your cross. When Jesus faced the cross it meant death; **when we face our cross it means life and abundance**. The cross you are to take up is found where your will/desire runs counter to God's will in your life. Jesus would say to you right now, "I have a gift for you if you will surrender to Me that part of your life that is not working—where we are at odds. I can reach that point of shame and pain and give you freedom."

You will be able to hear those words clearly when you understand that **every interaction with God is encased in grace.** That is why the Holy Spirit gets so excited about what God wants to give you; He is excited because the gift God gives you is victory over the enemy.

Remember, the enemy has nothing but contempt for you. Look at what he had to say about Job and all of mankind in the Old Testament:

> *Satan answered, "A human would do anything to save his life. But what do you think would happen if you reached down and took away his health? He'd curse you to your face, that's what."*
>
> Job 2:4-5 (MSG)

⇒ **Draw a picture showing how the enemy's schemes in the past have tried to dominate your life. Show what he has used as weapons against you.**

Satan is convinced that when push comes to shove, self-preservation will always rule in the hearts of men and women. He sees us as creatures completely run by fear, solely directed by our limbic system. The enemy has no way to predict what you will do if you aren't being driven by your own self-interests. **Satan can only forecast selfishness. He is helpless against a young woman who is living for a cause greater than herself.**

Your weapons against the enemy:

- *Deciding to allow God's Word to reign in your life rather than letting your feelings rule your life.*
- *Obeying God despite the difficulties you are going through.*
- *Doing what is right despite the costs.*
- *Facing your selfish desires and behaviors, then choosing not to be controlled by shame and fear, but instead accepting God's grace.*

⇒ **Which of those listed above are most difficult for you to walk in? Explain.**

_____

_____

_____

_____

There are some Biblical examples of how God has literally defeated the enemy by messing with his head. David did serious damage to his enemy Goliath. He literally messed with his enemy's head and disarmed the enemy.

> *Then David ran up to the Philistine and stood over him, pulled the giant's sword from its sheath, and finished the job by cutting off his head. When the Philistines saw that their great champion was dead, they scattered, running for their lives.*
>
> *David took the Philistine's head and brought it to Jerusalem. But the giant's weapons he placed in his own tent.*
>
> 1 Samuel 17:51, 54 (The Message)

The very thing that has led to such pain in your life can become the cutting edge of ministry to others in the future. Remember: If you scored six or more on the SAST (Sexual Addiction Screening Test) in Chapter 3, there is a stress fracture in your soul that the enemy is well aware of, and he will try to use it for your destruction. God wants to turn your ashes into beauty.

Look at another example of messing with the enemy's head In 1 Samuel. Israel treated the Ark of the Covenant like a good luck charm; as a result they lost it to the Philistines. They thought the physical Ark was their hope in battle rather than their obedience to and their relationship with God. After capturing the Ark, the Philistines placed it next to their god, Dagon.

> *But when the citizens of Ashdod went to see it the next morning, Dagon had fallen with his face to the ground in front of the Ark of the Lord! So they set the idol up again. But the next morning the same thing happened—the idol had fallen face down before the Ark of the Lord again. This time his head and hands had broken off and were lying in the doorway. Only the trunk of his body was left intact.*
> 1 Samuel 5:3-4 (NLT)

The reason we can mess with the enemy's head is because that is exactly what the Lord is doing all the time. He is messing with the enemy's head. It doesn't matter if the struggle is with a stone idol or pornographic or romantic idols.

How can you mess with the enemy's head in your battle? Here are some great suggestions:

1. *Learn to affirm yourself and take care of yourself. Learn to look in your Heavenly Father's eyes and see who you really are.* Those who struggle with behavior that substitutes intensity for intimacy are terrible at caring for themselves. This is why they find themselves in such pain and acting out once again. To underline how God really sees you refer to "Who I am in Christ" in the *Resources* section of this book.

2. *Learn from your mistakes.* Once you realize you are the apple of His eye, you will learn from your mistakes rather than punish yourself for your mistakes.

3. *Connect with those who know your story . . . and know what really matters in life.* Your greatest enemy is isolation; significant meaning is only found in community.

4. *Allow pain, joy, fear, and anger in your life.* You must become an expert at identifying your own feelings; practice being mentally, emotionally, and physically present rather than isolating, fantasizing, or medicating. The page of emotions/feelings in the *Resources* section can help you identify your feelings.

> **Turn now to the Emotions/Feelings page in the *Resources* section and write down some of the feelings you are now experiencing.**

_____

_____

_____

5. *It is crucial that you develop healthy boundaries with self and others.* Healthy boundaries are critical in helping develop a safe life.

☙ Which of these five suggestions can you immediately begin to incorporate into your life?

_____

☙ How might incorporating these suggestions in your life help you unravel the plans of the enemy?

_____

_____

_____

Instead of yielding to fearful, angry or lustful thoughts, you can remain in a spirit of thankfulness, gratitude and praise. Practicing a **spirit of worship and praise will disarm the enemy and his tactics in your life.** That is why one of the most powerful forms of worship is to walk as David did. He is very clear about his struggles; he didn't deny the negative. Yet at the same time he declared that there is a higher level of truth than just the difficulties he was presently facing. Most of David's psalms were powerful declarations of praise.

> *They have tracked me down, they now surround me, with eyes alert, to throw me to the ground.*
> *They are like a lion hungry for prey, like a great lion crouching in cover.*
> *Rise up, O Lord, confront them, bring them down; rescue me from the wicked by your sword.*
> Psalm 17:11-13 (NIV)

Now notice the profound declaration of praise that David fires right at the enemy.

> *And me? I plan on looking you full in the face. When I get up, I'll see your full stature and live heaven on earth.*
> Psalm 17:15 (The Message)

Cindy wrote a beautiful psalm of lament as she grieved over what had been stolen in her life and how her heart had been deceived. It was pages long by the time she was through with this personal psalm that transparently described her pain, sorrow and God's triumph in her life.

☙ Write a beginning of your own original psalm in the space below. It may include your present struggle, the negative issues, and/or declaring a higher level of truth, and a declaration of praise to God. Please continue on your own paper or in your own time as your heart cries out to God.

_____

_____

_____

_____

_____

There is much New Testament truth in David's Psalm. Somehow he understood that God empathizes with us, He doesn't just sympathize with us. The New Testament book of Hebrews speaks of Christ's ability to sympathize with our weaknesses. Sympathy is the ability to feel sorrow for another's misfortune. Christ is totally capable of that. However, His ultimate goal is greater than feeling sorry for our misfortunes. If we are in Christ, nothing of misfortune befalls us; our lives are "Father-filtered." God uses everything to develop us into the person He has called us to be. Amazingly, David understood that fact.

Empathy is different than sympathy in that it says, "I know what you are going through. Stick with it because even the tough times are in God's hands." After you walk with God for a while, you begin to realize the central fact of the cross: **You have to die to live.** God allows the tough times to come into our lives to stretch us past our definition of success to our destiny. That is what David was declaring (and we can, too!): "When I come through this, when I get back on my feet, I will be changed by Your loving hand into the person I cry to be. And in the process I will come to know You as never before. I will begin to grasp the full dimensions of Your awesomeness. Therefore, I will stand in this difficult place until I see the fulfillment of what You have spoken over me."

God has given us promises about being overcomers but those promises cannot be accessed without obedience to the cross. At the end of this chapter you will be involved in a very important exercise that will enable you to specifically identify your cross with respect to your romantic and sexual battles.

Before we take on that exercise, we need to identify the fiery darts the enemy has been using against you in the form of thoughts, difficulties and problems that have troubled you.

> *...above all take up the shield of faith with which you will be able to quench all the fiery darts of the wicked one.*
>
> Ephesians 6:24 (NKJ)

Allow the Holy Spirit to quicken you with His wisdom as to how you can move in faith in the opposite direction. Remember, choosing to walk in obedience to the cross disarms the enemy.

Defeating the Assaults from Hell

The Enemy's Fiery Darts	Your Obedience to the Cross
Example: You will never be able to stop your out-of-control behavior	I have worked my way through this book with other young women who are struggling; I will finish this process and experience victory.

Having a clear target in life is crucial. It is a life or death matter in winning your battle with romantic and sexual bondage. In the previous chapters, we have repeatedly helped you identify the places where you are uniquely vulnerable. Doing the next exercise will give you a *very clear picture* of the trigger points and beliefs in your life that cripple you. You can only win this battle if you are willing to identify and walk out what you identify in the three circles.

Three Circles[64]

The **Three Circles** graphic is designed to give you a very clear and convenient method of displaying all you have discovered so far. It will be an invaluable aid in understanding your masks and how to live authentically. The explanation of the circles is followed by the actual graphic of the circles. You will be asked to write your own information in the circles based on what you learn from the explanation and examples.

The **INNER CIRCLE** has a cross for a very important reason. This describes the place where you need to die to self, where your will and God's will for you are at odds. **This is your abstinence list.** This is the place where you must choose to abstain, where you chose to die to self. I call it the "foxhole" in my life. When I am engaging in these behaviors and involved in these kinds of thought processes, it is like I am inviting danger into my life and valuing the temporary intensity rather than investing into the permanent intimacy. Here is where the enemy has a deadly weapon and I don't. In other words, I am in serious trouble.

Inside the inner circle, write down the compulsive, self-defeating activities from which you must abstain. Abstinence is one day at a time. God is asking you to walk in purity and keep your mind pure TODAY by His grace. I call it the "manna" principle. When God led Israel out of the bondage of Egypt, He supplied them with the food they needed one day at a time. God will provide the grace you need one day at a time but you have to know where to apply it, thus the priority of the inner circle.

If you go back and read the story of Israel's deliverance in Exodus, specifically chapters seven through ten, you would discover a fascinating phenomenon. Initially, the plagues that God brought upon the land hit both the Egyptians and Israelites. But by the fourth plague things changed. God declared that He would make a distinction between His people and the Egyptians. All the rest of the plagues don't hit the camp of the Israelites.

I find it interesting that initially the plagues hit the just and the unjust. As followers of Christ we can't escape difficulties in this life and you definitely can't medicate them away. Our faith doesn't insulate us from problems but, on the other hand, there is what I call a "corporate anointing."

A Holy Spirit anointing enables you to walk differently in this world. My point from Exodus is you usually find the grace you need to walk in purity when you are in relationship in the community of faith.

Your *Behind the Mask* group is an absolute lifeline for you. You will want to share the result of this exercise with them in detail. Listen carefully to their input and suggestions because you usually have a very incomplete understanding of yourself and the battle you are facing.

Your **INNER CIRCLE** might include comments like:
- *No masturbation*
- *No viewing of erotic sites or porn*

- *No touching or fingering between me and my boyfriend below the neckline*
- *No sexting*
- *No medicating of my feelings of loneliness or worthlessness*
- *No surfing of TV alone, secretly looking for sexual excitement*
- *No alcohol or drugs*

Next is the **MIDDLE CIRCLE**. These are the "triggers" that lead you into the hellish situations where you find yourself living trapped behind your mask and functioning in systems of shame. The middle circle includes those behaviors that fall between the devastating compulsive behavior that totally demoralize you and the healthy sexuality you truly cry for in Christ. These are called the "trip wires" in your life. The enemy is crafty. The trip wires furthest out give you an objective indicator that your adversary is drawing near.

These **MIDDLE CIRCLE** behaviors will eventually lead us back into the INNER CIRCLE if we don't develop strong boundaries and stay in touch with the fact that we are powerless over our compulsions. In this circle list people, places, situations, things that you must avoid because they trigger you. (Refer back to your FASTER Scale if needed.) List mental "slippery slopes."

Your **Middle Circle activities** might include:
- *Feeling bored, angry, isolated or frustrated with your life*
- *Lying, blaming, rationalizing, justifying or omitting certain facts when asked*
- *Flirting at school or at the gym with the idea of hooking up*
- *Going to parties where alcohol is being served or drinking/ doing drugs with friends*
- *Surfing the web looking for unhealthy sites*
- *Texting with suggestive sexual or erotic comments*
- *Watching R-rated or X-rated movies*
- *Cursing*
- *Spending too much alone time with a boyfriend in secluded places*
- *Hanging with young adults who don't have your values*

Finally, the **OUTER CIRCLE** needs to be described. Write activities here that support your healing and also describe what healthy sexual boundaries look like for you. The question of healthy sexual boundaries can be a real puzzle for someone who has been struggling with romantic and sexual bondage. Usually when I ask young women to describe what healthy sexual boundaries are, they give me a blank stare. But it is vitally important that you think this through because if your only goal is to stop your past behavior, you are defeated before you start. You must have a vivid picture of what your dreams and hopes are for your future. Otherwise, you will lack the passion and courage to win the war within yourself.

Your **OUTER CIRCLE** activities might include:
- *Faithfully doing my homework in this book for my group meetings*
- *Read and process books on healthy boundaries and dating*
- *Learn to listen to myself and respect myself enough to set some strong sexual boundaries*
- Create and be accountable for new healthy dating habits and boundaries
- *Explore new healthy hobbies and interests in my life*
- *Develop relationships with healthy Christian women I admire*
- *Put safeguards on all my electronics—phones and computers. (Covenant Eyes is recommended)*
- *Be totally honest in all of my dealings and admit when I am wrong*
- *Develop healthy peer friendships with women who also desire a Christ-centered life*

- *Develop a meaningful and deep devotional life*
- *Learn not to focus on "all or nothing" in life but to do something healthy every day*
- *Develop healthy eating habits and a workout routine*
- *Learn how to really relax when needed*
- *Work on a healthy relationship with my parents*
- *Use the FASTER scale daily to become more self-aware*

Three Circles Exercise Example

Inner Circle = abstinence behaviors; my cross. **Middle Circle** = trigger behaviors or activities to avoid
Outer Circle = describes healthy sexuality for me & lists activities/behaviors that support my healing

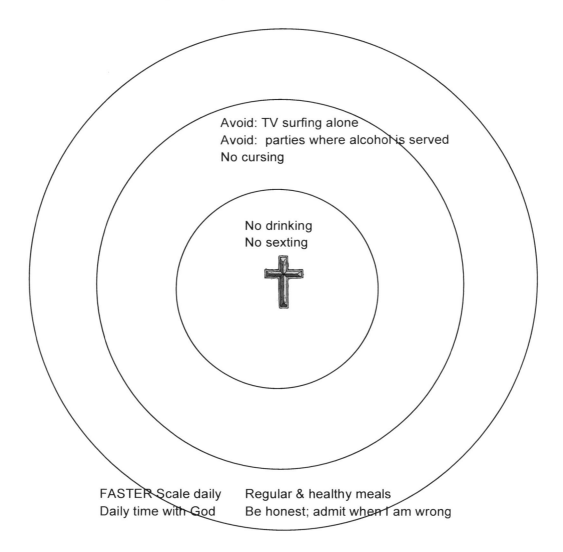

  Complete the **Three Circles** exercise now using the diagram provided on the next page. Remember—this is a document in progress. At least <u>once every three to six months</u> you should revisit this exercise and adjust your responses to your current level of healing and understanding. You will find that this is an excellent indicator of the progress you have made and an invaluable tool in understanding your struggles.

My Three Circles Exercise[65]

Inner Circle = abstinence behaviors; my cross
Middle Circle = trigger behaviors or activities to avoid
Outer Circle = describes healthy sexuality for me & lists activities/behaviors that support my healing

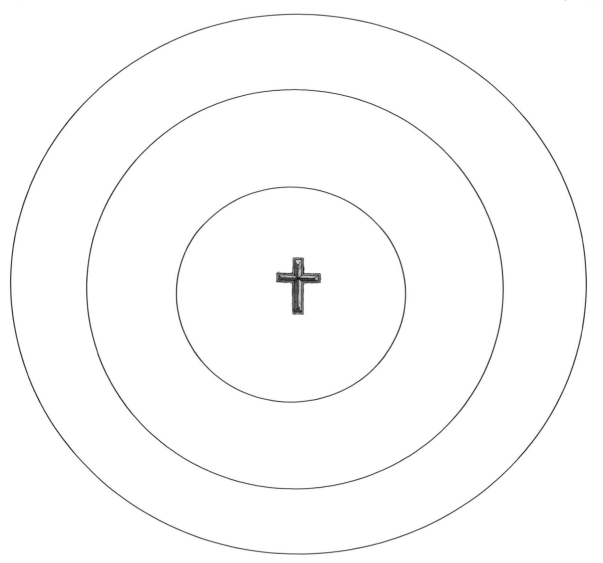

Date I completed this exercise: _____

Date I will review/evaluate my responses & adjust for my current level of healing:

_____

> ✎ You have identified those things that will encourage a healthy lifestyle (the outer circle). Now write out a prayer asking the Holy Spirit to help you on a daily basis to walk in these patterns that will form healthy habits.

_____

_____

_____

_____

_____

_____

_____

_____

_____

_____

> ✎ Who will you ask to hold you accountable for this commitment?

_____

Assignment: Complete the next chapter.

> **Song recommendation for meditation this week:**
> ## The Anthem
> ### by Jake Hamilton

Chapter 12
Unmasking Healthy Boundaries

Ellen

People do stupid, unhealthy things, especially in survival mode. That is where I have been most of my life.

I recently found out I had been molested at ten months of age. Two different uncles, two different cousins, and my stepdad sexually abused me over the years. I grew to believe I was made for sex. At age seven I started masturbating any time I felt stress and believed this compulsive desire for sexual release kept me from going insane. Since the age of five I have had a boyfriend. I remember at an early age using kisses and hand-holding to control my "boyfriends." Once I learned how to control a boy, I did it whenever I felt it suited my purposes.

In my teens, sex became my weapon of choice. Looking back now, I realize I became exactly what each guy wanted so I could optimize the way in which my needs were met. Today I can see how wrong it was and I am sorry for those choices. I was in survival mode and that is where I have been most of my life. I know I can't keep living this way.

———————————

Ellen has been in survival mode and vulnerable since she was a baby. Her caregivers didn't protect her, so she felt vulnerable with no sense of security. Some in this situation become extremely accommodating to unhealthy relationships and either use sex to try to control or they have a hard time setting limits and are unable to say "no."

Since she was young Jessica also has been in survival mode due to emotional neglect, and feels vulnerable and accommodates to others through codependent relationships.

Jessica

All I want is to know I am loved no matter who I am or what I do, but deep inside me I do not believe that I am. Many conversations with my mom leave me feeling "less than" and worthless. I am driven by fear of saying the wrong thing or upsetting her, so I give her access to every area of my life. Every time I make a decision, I wonder what my mom would think of it even though I am in college! Her voice plays in my head stronger than any other voice, including my own. We talk every other day for an hour-and-a-half. You would think we were best friends, but I resent that I have let her have so much control over me. I feel helpless and ashamed that she is so much a part of my thought process. This has bled into my relationship with my boyfriend; I don't feel like I have a voice in what we spend our money on or what we do together. I can't tell when his thoughts end or where mine begin. I hate that I do this to myself, but I have no idea how to stop letting others live my life for me or define who I am!

———————————

❧ **Is there any part of Ellen's or Jessica's testimony to which you can relate? Explain.**

_____

_____

_____

_____

Part of moving towards "healthy" for those caught in the cycle of compulsive behavior is to create new rituals. Learning to set boundaries is a tool we can use to begin to walk in health.

Where are you when it comes to boundaries? How hard is it for you to be healthy in this area? The following questions will help you think through your present rituals when it comes to boundaries.

❧ **Write your answers to the following questions**.

1. On a scale of 1 to 10 (ten being the most difficult), how difficult is it for you to feel like a loving person and set healthy boundaries at the same time? Circle one:

1   2   3   4   5   6   7   8   9   10

least difficult   most difficult

2. What is a boundary? In a sentence or two, describe a boundary.

_____

_____

_____

_____

3. How do you feel if someone is upset because of a boundary you have set (such as a boyfriend, relative or close friend, guys you are dating)?

_____

_____

_____

4. How do you feel when you need to set limits with someone who is close to you? Consider your level of fear, guilt, shame, panic, and anger.

_____

_____

_____

5. Do you believe boundaries are selfish?   Why or why not?

_____

_____

_____

_____

6. How do you feel when others close to you tell you "no"?

_____

_____

7. Do you try to change someone's mind to get what you want? If so, give an example.

_____

_____

_____

_____

8. What does Jesus/ the Bible say about boundaries?

_____

_____

_____

_____

Usually those struggling with compulsive sexual behavior have little, if any, understanding of healthy boundaries because of what was done to them and what they have done to others. That is why it is important to have a biblical perspective on what Jesus says about boundaries. The Cloud & Townsend book *Boundaries* gives us a great biblical definition of what boundaries are and are not.

> In short, boundaries are not walls. The Bible does not say that we are to be "walled off" from others; in fact, it says that we are to be one with them (John 17:11). We are to be in community with them. But in every community, all members have their own space and property. The important thing is that property lines are permeable enough to allow passing and strong enough to keep out danger. Often, when people are abused while growing up, they reverse the function of boundaries and keep the bad in and the good out.[66]

One of the best pictures illustrating healthy boundaries versus shame-based boundaries is illustrated with a zipper metaphor in the book, *Facing Shame*.[67] The author explains how shame-based people have zippers on the outside of their lives and anyone can have access to those zippers. Healthy people have zippers on the inside of their lives and they control who has access.

🔖 **Can you think of a time where this illustration of the zipper would be true in your life?**

Example of zipper on the inside where you had control:

_____

_____

Example of zipper on the outside where others took control:

_____

_____

Revelation 3:20 (NASB) shows that Jesus respects our boundaries:

> ***Behold, I stand at the door and knock; if anyone hears My voice and opens the door, I will come in to him, and will dine with him, and he with Me.***

Maybe you have seen this concept beautifully illustrated in the picture of Jesus knocking at a door that has no knob on the outside. The door can only be opened from the inside. God has given you control over your relationship with Him. You choose when to let Him in and how much you want to yield to Him.

God has also designed you for relationship with others and He desires that you have healthy boundaries in place. As stated in the Cloud & Townsend definition, boundaries are not designed to keep people out. In fact, those who have appropriate boundaries actually increase their ability to care about others.

For example, if Jessica had boundaries with her mom, she would be free to see herself as a distinct person from her mother. Her love for her mom would be real and not forced by codependency.

Ellen is afraid of real intimacy because most of her life she has either been a victim of others or she has used power over others to feel safe and meet her needs. If she faces her fear of letting others in who are safe and realizes she has power to keep out those who are not, she can begin to find real intimacy.

Jesus was the most compassionate and caring person that ever lived. Yet Jesus had healthy boundaries in place that released Him to care effectively for people. Let's look at some scriptures from Mark that show how Jesus repeatedly set boundaries to take care of His own needs and those of His twelve disciples.

Mark 1:33-37:
The whole town gathered...Jesus healed many...Very early...Jesus got up, left the house and went to a solitary place...and when they found Him they exclaimed, "Everyone is looking for you!

Mark 1:45:
Jesus could no longer enter a town openly but stayed outside in lonely places.

☙ **What do these Bible descriptions tell us about Jesus' personal boundaries and how he tried to take care of himself?**

_____

_____

Mark 3:13:
He called to those He wanted...He appointed twelve.

Mark 5:18:
The man...begged to go with Him. Jesus did not let him...

Mark 5:37:
He did not let anyone follow Him except...

Mark 9:30:
Jesus did not want anyone to know where they were, because He was teaching His disciples.

These scriptures clearly show Jesus' decision to limit and/or give access to people.

☙ **What are the implications for your life as you see Jesus limiting access or giving access to people in His life?**

_____

_____

_____

Mark 3:7-9:
He told them to have a small boat ready for Him, and to keep the people from crowding Him.

☙ **What does this Scripture infer about the balance of having friends help us when we have needs?**

_____

_____

_____

Notice that in caring for others Jesus also recognized His need to care for Himself. He withdrew and even said "no" in order to be effective and remain healthy. He made requests and did not meet every demand made of Him. In fact, when Jesus became the sacrifice for our sins, He made it clear it was His decision.[68]

> *For this reason the Father loves Me, because I lay down My life that I may take it again. No one has taken it away from Me, but I lay it down on My own initiative.*
> John 10:17-18 (NAS)

When we find ourselves doing things to get people to like us or end up performing for approval, affirmation, or identity we can easily slip into allowing others to set our boundaries for us.

Cindy, from previous chapters, also gave up boundaries over her own body to get approval from men.

Cindy

My clothing was part of the mask that I wore to cover the pain inside me. Looking back after my healing process, I am appalled that I wanted to wear THAT tank top without anything else under it, or THAT skirt without some kind of leggings. I wanted attention. I deeply desired to be loved by men. My sister would always say, "Cindy, you're wearing THAT?" I thought she was just being overly protective, but I can see now that I made decisions in my wardrobe selections with the motive to get attention from men. Everything inside me wanted to have major sex appeal. I found great comfort in knowing that I could turn a guy's head, or that he would think of me sexually. I didn't know why I wanted that; I just didn't see anything wrong with flaunting what I've got.

> **Share about a time you relinquished your boundary in order to gain approval or affirmation.**

_____

_____

_____

_____

> **Describe a time when you reluctantly said "yes," agreeing to something or committing to something you later regretted.**

_____

_____

_____

_____

> **Write about a time when you over-extended yourself and suffered as a result.**

_____

_____

_____

> **Share about a time when you said yes to your compulsive behavior and suffered the results.**

_____

_____

_____

_____

❧ After looking at how Jesus responded in such a way that He balanced the needs of others with His own needs, what imbalances can you see with respect to your life and your relationships?

_____

_____

_____

_____

_____

❧ What is your greatest challenge in setting healthy boundaries?

_____

_____

_____

_____

_____

❧ What early childhood experiences might have caused you to believe that the "zipper" in your life needed to be on the outside, giving anyone and everyone access?

_____

_____

_____

_____

_____

_____

_____

❧ **Draw a picture showing how inappropriate access to your life has affected you.**

✎ **Make a list of <u>people who have had too much access</u> to your life and the repercussions or consequences for you.**

NAME OF PERSON	REPERCUSSIONS/ CONSEQUENCES

✎ **Make a list of <u>people whose boundaries you may have overstepped</u> and the consequences for you and them.**

NAME OF PERSON	REPERCUSSIONS/ CONSEQUENCES

✎ **Make a list of people with whom you have seen good boundaries. Next to each person's name write down how that person's good boundaries or your own good boundaries with that person affected you and your relationship.**

NAME OF PERSON	BENEFITS/ RESULTS
Example: My parents	Although my parents have put dating rules in place, they are interested in my input & consider my opinions.

Since most women are not getting married until their middle twenties, a large part of caring for yourself would be to set some healthy boundaries for dating, especially during those times you find yourself wrestling with deep passions and a longing for independence from your parents. Studies of the brain have found that it is almost impossible to stop doing something compulsive, especially for young adults whose impulse control center (the prefrontal cortex) is not fully developed. But, they have also found that when you plan something positive it is easier to follow through.

Create a plan to walk in victory and health!

1. Identify your sexual limits before dating. If you are already in a committed dating situation, share your values and limits with your boyfriend.

One gal I (Diane) was counseling had made some very destructive dating choices. After she took some healing classes and went through counseling, I asked her to make a list of what healthy dating now looks like to her. She came up with a great list of limits based on her new-found relationship with Christ. She presented them to her new boyfriend who said he didn't like those limits. I knew she had experienced great healing when she challenged him with this statement: "What on this list don't I deserve? This list reflects my values to walk in purity and my desire to be respected." *She loved herself enough to expect respect.* I was proud of her for her new choices to date only those who would love her and her values.

2. Look at a young man's spiritual commitment.

Check out your boyfriend's spiritual commitment. Don't be afraid to ask him about his beliefs. Clinical studies reveal that spirituality is an important factor in shaping adolescent sexual attitudes and behaviors. Teens who describe themselves as spiritual and see their faith as an important part of their lives are much less likely to engage in any form of inappropriate sexual behavior. The pattern is especially strong among adolescents who regularly attend religious services.[69]

3. Share your commitment to purity with your parents.

A large body of scientific research indicates that adolescents want to hear from their parents on issues related to sexuality. Sharing your commitment opens the door for discussion, and you can also learn more about your parents' attitudes and expectations about sexuality.[70]

4. Share your plan and be accountable to a mentor or someone in your group.

A gal who was in one of our groups had been out of control sexually all through her teens and early twenties. She committed to being accountable to one of the young women in the group. This young woman would call her friend before and after the date to let her know she had followed through on her limits. I asked her if being in her late twenties made it hard to keep this accountability commitment. I will never forget her comment:

"During my growing up years my parents didn't care who I dated or what I did. As a result, I suffered the effects of having an abortion. I feel so blessed that I have friends that love me enough to call me and keep me accountable; I wish my parents had cared as much as my friends do now."

Create & Use a Dating Plan!

✓ **Identify your sexual limits.**

✓ **Look at the spiritual commitment of anyone you want to date.**

✓ **Share your commitment to purity with your parents.**

✓ **Share your plan & be accountable to a mentor or someone in your *Behind the Mask* group.**

---

5. Complete your dating plan; be prepared to share it with your group.[71]

My Dating Plan

My commitment to draw the line sexually (expressed in my own words):

Signature _____ Date _____

What are my limits sexually?

1.

2.

3.

4.

What is my target in this relationship? What do I hope to learn? What do I want to experience?

1.

2.

3.

When will I share my dating plan with my boyfriend?

How will I share it?

When will we talk with our parents?

If our parents will not support our commitment to purity, what other adult friends or mentors will we talk to instead?

One or two female accountability friends.

_____   _____

Jessica decided years later, after she was married, to set boundaries with her mom in order to establish herself as her own distinct person.

Jessica

"With the counselor's advice, I decided to take a six month break from communicating with my parents in order to establish my independence. It might sound crazy, but it was the scariest thing I have ever done in my life! With the support of my husband and counselors, I learned to be the woman I never knew I was. I cried myself to sleep the day I emailed my parents about my decision to stop communicating. I was terrified to live life without their voices in my head. I felt incapable to stand on my own two feet, and was scared that I might die without them to make decisions for me. Learning that I can survive the first day of school without my mom's advice built in me an inner confidence I never knew I had. In the following months I learned that I could plan parties, decorate my home, take care of my daughter, and take care of my husband and myself without her voice in my head. It took me months to hear and trust my own voice, but I am a new woman today. I have found security in listening to the Holy Spirit and trusting my gut rather than always having to lean on others for advice. Now I have boundaries in my conversations with mom, and I can honestly say that she is a good friend to me. I am enjoying who she is and delighting in our differences."

The kind of commitment to health that Jessica made might also be important for someone who feels enmeshed in a relationship with a boyfriend or family member. Taking a break from an unhealthy relationship may allow you to discover who YOU really are, and discover that you can take care of yourself without a guy. Every young woman has a unique identity distinct from that of anyone else. One fabulous part of being a young woman is the opportunity to grow into an independent and capable person. If that growth process is meddled with through codependent relationships, your emotional growth may be stunted.

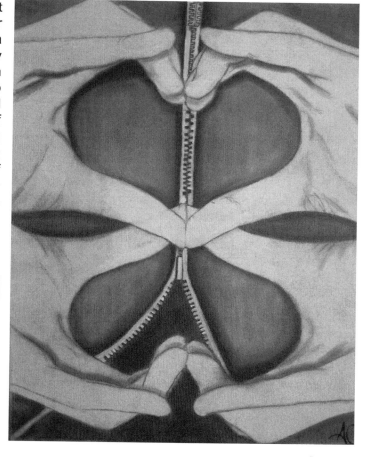

> ***The Struggle***
> By Angela Hutson-Cumpston
>
> Boundaries:
> Zipper pull—inside or outside?
> (Inside= you decide your boundaries
> & who has access to your heart)

For young women still living at home, boundaries with parents may look different than Jessica's boundaries she set with her mom later in her life. If you live at home and are under the age of 18, it may be best to respect the rules of your parents or guardian (exceptions include abusive situations, where you would need to find safety first and seek professional help).

If (or when) you are over 18 and continue to live at home, it is important to negotiate new rules with your parents while still respecting the fact that you are under their roof. If you are in a situation where you think you may be under the unhealthy control of a parent, we would encourage you to trust your gut and seek other safe people with whom to relate. When Jessica was living in her parents' home, she often consulted with her best friend's mom to get an objective perspective when she knew her own mom would criticize rather than listen.

  Since learning to set healthy boundaries is such an important new step in your healing, write a prayer asking God to open your heart and mind to begin to see boundaries from His perspective. Let Him know in your own words any struggles you might have in making changes in this area of your life.

_____

_____

_____

_____

_____

_____

_____

_____

_____

_____

Assignment: Complete the next lesson.

Song recommendation for meditation this week:
Slow Your Breath Down
by Future of Forestry

Chapter 13
Unveiling Masked Emotions

Anna (mentioned in previous chapters) was violently abused sexually as a young girl and not protected by those who were supposed to protect her. When she was a teenager, Anna's father lost his job and her family became homeless. She and her family lived in a tent at campgrounds near her town while her father looked for work. This experience of unmet needs and lack of safety and security triggered past memories of coping in times of stress. Anna spiraled toward destructive behaviors again. She found herself using drugs to feel accepted and to cope with her pain.

Another young woman, Peggy, also found herself spiraling toward destructive behaviors when past abuse was triggered.

Peggy

Every time my father comes into town I start drinking right before his arrival. I sometimes even act out sexually. I have begun to see the pattern and am wondering if his inappropriate sexual contact in my growing up years is triggering this pattern. I have been unable to confront him with the past and I get angry every time he wants to get together. Since I am a Christian, I feel like I need to honor him as my parent as Scripture commands in Deuteronomy 5:16.

As you will remember, we discovered that trauma drives much of our compulsive behavior. Peggy's inability to reconcile her past, especially with her father, continues to trigger her compulsive behavior. She brings up a good point about honoring your parents and I have often heard that reasoning in the counseling office. The balance point is Matthew 18 where Jesus warns about the consequences of harming a child:

> **But whoever causes one of these little ones who believes in Me to sin, it would be better for him if a millstone were hung around his neck, and he were drowned in the depth of the sea.**
>
> Matthew 18: 6 (NKJ)

Jesus spoke harsh words to those who would harm and defile these little ones, those who would rob them of their innocence and trusting, child-like heart.

The only way Peggy and Anna will be able to stop the compulsive triggers is to face the hurt and anger from their past. Like most struggling with compulsive behavior, they have developed coping mechanisms as ways to mask and bury the anger. When stress, fear, and/or tension build up, they immediately move into a cycle of destructive behavior to avoid and ignore their pain and anger.

By definition, anger is an emotional state that varies in intensity from mild irritation to intense fury and rage.[72] Anger can be caused by external events: hurt from a relationship experience, unmet expectations, things that don't go your way, etc. Anger resulting from internal events can be more difficult to identify because it is based on a person's internal belief system, reactions to situations, inner voice, and value systems. Anger is also a physical response that activates and increases adrenaline in your body, which is why physical ailments often result.

☙ **Please take some time to evaluate your reactions and responses for situations that may result in anger. Is each statement true or false for you? Circle your answers.**

ANGER TEST[73]

T F   1. I concern myself with others' opinions of me more than I would like to admit.
T F   2. I have had relationships with others that could be described as stormy or unstable.
T F   3. It seems like I end up helping others more than they help me.
T F   4. I sometimes wonder how much my friends or family members accept me.
T F   5. I realize I don't like to admit to myself how angry I feel.
T F   6. Sometimes I use humor to avoid facing my feelings or to keep others from knowing how I really feel.
T F   7. Sometimes when I feel angry, I find myself doing things I know are wrong.
T F   8. I like having times when no one knows what I am doing.
T F   9. I usually don't tell people when I feel hurt.
T F 10. At times, I wish I had more friends.
T F 11. Criticism bothers me a great deal.
T F 12. I desire acceptance from others but fear rejection.
T F 13. I worry a lot about my relationships with others.
T F 14. I believe I am overly sensitive to rejection.
T F 15. I have often felt inferior to others.
T F 16. Often I say "yes" and am upset at myself for not saying "no."
T F 17. Even though I don't like it, there are times when I wear a mask in social settings.
T F 18. I don't seem to have the emotional support I would like from my family and friends.
T F 19. I would like to tell people exactly what I think.
T F 20. There are times I feel inadequate in the way I handle personal relationships.
T F 21. My conscience bothers me about things I have done in the past.
T F 22. Sometimes it seems my religious life is more of a burden than a help.
T F 23. There are times that I would like to run away from home.
T F 24. I have had too many quarrels or disagreements with members of my family.
T F 25. I have been disillusioned with love.
T F 26. I try controlling my weight in unhealthy ways.
T F 27. I have a challenge controlling sexual fantasies.
T F 28. To be honest, I prefer to find someone else to blame my problems on.
T F 29. My greatest struggles are within myself.
T F 30. Other people find more fault with me than they really should.
T F 31. I find myself saying things that I shouldn't have said.
T F 32. My decisions are often governed by my feelings.
T F 33. When something irritates me I find it hard to calm down quickly.
T F 34. I consider myself to be possessive in my personal relationships.
T F 35. Sometimes I could be described as moody.

Please take a moment now to review your answers, being truthful with yourself.

Guide to the Anger Test

🕭 How many of the 35 statements did you answer True? _____

Your score (the <u>total</u> number of statements marked **True**) indicates the following about you and anger:

    1-19   Normal range
    20-29 Needs and/or circumstances are pressing
    30+   May need help through counseling for trauma or specific issues

Note: A score less than 30 may also indicate issues best handled through counseling.

Anna and Peggy would have scored high on the Anger Test, but both expressed their anger in different ways. Anna held a lot of her anger inside and repressed it (anger turned inward). Peggy, on the other hand, was explosive with her anger (anger turned outward.).

🕭 Circle the responses that best typify your anger.[74]

REPRESSED ANGER	EXPLOSIVE ANGER
1. Very easily hurt	1. Critical and Cutting
2. Afraid to say "no"	2. Never listen to others viewpoints
3. Feel everything is my fault	3. Must be the best
4. Feel used "doormat" mentality	4. Demand own rights
5. Usually a loner, a form of hiding	5. Argumentative
6. Easily depressed	6. Lack compassion
7. Do not know how to have fun	7. Self-centered and judgmental
8. Usually fearful	8. Hold grudges

🕭 Look at those you circled and then share a recent incident when your anger was repressed or explosive.

_____

_____

_____

_____

🕭 Since anger is a secondary emotion, what fear were you facing in that situation that caused you to become angry? (fear of rejection, fear of being hurt, devalued, etc.)

_____

_____

_____

_____

Repressed anger turns inward causing depression, self-pity, and low self-esteem. It often leads to bitterness. Explosive anger turns outward, attacks others, and also leads to bitterness. Neither response is healthy, yet both are normal human responses to hurt.

Repressed anger
Emotions are part of us. Each time we repress them, they become like bricks on a protective wall inside of us. We hide behind the wall and put on a mask to protect ourselves from harm. Anger is often one of the feelings least safe to express. Therefore, it is frequently repressed.

Unresolved anger can be a shackle or a burden too heavy to carry. So many of us, like Peggy, are weighted down by this burden without realizing it. Scripture says be angry but don't sin and don't let the sun go down on your anger (Ephesians 4:26-27). Therefore, anger is not a sin, but if we allow it to be carried into the next day and the next, it becomes a burden. We are created to carry only one day's worth of anger.

So how do we get out of this cycle of anger and deal honestly with our past hurts?

  Read Steps One and Two then list your responses in the chart that follows Step Two.

Step One: Identify people who have hurt you.
To help you create this list, review Chapters 6, 7 and 8, specifically noting your Wounded Heart, PTSI scores, and past hurts identified in your grievance story. Include people from your past who engender feelings of hurt or anger, how they hurt you, and your relationship with them in the present.

Step Two: Identify Emotions:
Under the column titled "Feelings" identify the emotions that lie beneath the anger. The continued story of Peggy might help you get in touch with some of your feelings:

Peggy

It took a couple of months to dissect the anger I was feeling about my dad. I realized my dad wasn't the first person who made me feel shame over what had happened. At 15, a boyfriend raped me. At first I felt guilty because we had overstepped my boundaries. Now I realize that my "no" was a "no" and he violated my boundary. I was angry at the shame I have felt over something I didn't want. I was angry that he dropped me once he got what he wanted. I was angry he lied, manipulated, and used me like an object rather than a person. I was angry that he used me for his own pleasure. I questioned God, "Where were you? Why didn't you stop him?" I have felt lonely, embarrassed, ashamed, and abandoned by God, my boyfriend and my dad. The sorrow of what happened fills my soul and I am afraid I will always feel this loneliness. I realize that my fear of being alone drives my addiction to act out with men.

Identifying My Past Hurts

Person who hurt me	Description of the hurt	My current relationship with that person	Feelings (See Feelings/Emotions chart—Resources section)
Peggy's Example: dad	I drink to numb pain from him molesting me	Avoid being around him	Fear my dad
Peggy's Example: boyfriend	Fearful to tell anyone of rape	Avoid him & his friends	Lonely, embarrassed, violated, ashamed

Step 3: Write a letter

Write a letter (not necessarily to be sent) for each person you listed in the chart. State the hurt that was engendered by their actions and the emotions you have felt as a result. Allow your anger to be expressed. One young woman shared, "As I wrote, I felt like all the anger in my heart was flowing out, down my arm, and through the pen I used to write the letter." Remember, Scripture says: be angry but don't sin. In other words express your anger in a way that will bring health to you.

> ✑ **Take time to write a letter to each person on your list. The letters are for your healing, and may or may not be sent. We recommend that you finish this chapter before making any decisions about whether or not to send your letters. Also, consult your *Behind the Mask* leader or group, or a trusted adult or counselor before actually sending any letters.**

Step 4: Make a decision to forgive.

Some may cringe when they come to this step, as forgiveness may seem like condoning the behavior that caused you pain. Read on as we explore biblical forgiveness.

Let's look at forgiveness on two fronts: forgiving those who have created trauma in our lives and forgiving ourselves for our own behavior. Working through forgiveness will not be easy; in fact it is part of the hard work that recovery requires. Forgiving and being forgiven require new understanding and courage. You may have been taught that being a Christian requires you to forgive and forget.

→ **What have you been taught about forgiveness?**

_____

_____

_____

_____

Myths about Forgiveness

What does Scripture actually say? Some of what we have been taught was based on personal experiences and is not biblical truth. Looking at the myths can help us more clearly define biblical forgiveness.

Forgiveness does NOT mean...

Myth # 1: **I must approve of what was done to me.**
Myth # 2: **I must ignore what was done to me.**
An officer struck Jesus when he was brought before the high priest (John 18:19-23). Jesus did not approve of or ignore what the officer did and questioned him, *"If I have spoken evil, bear witness of the evil; but if well, why do you strike Me?"* (John 18:23 NKJ)

Myth # 3: **I must pretend that I am not hurt.**
In the John 18 Scripture mentioned above, Jesus addressed the hurt and confronted the man who struck him rather than pretending it didn't hurt.

Myth # 4: **I must forget what was done to me.**
After Moses asks God to forgive the people of Israel (Numbers 14), God replied, *"I have forgiven them as you asked. Nevertheless...."* and God goes on to explain the consequences that would still occur because of their sins. So even God did not "forgive and forget." They were forgiven yet they would still suffer the consequences for those sins. It's an example of the spiritual Law of Sowing and Reaping that governs our world. It is God's way of teaching us cause and effect in relationships.

Myth # 5: I must reconcile with the person who has hurt me.
The Bible clearly shows us we always need to forgive. God forgave the whole world and yet the whole world is not reconciled to him (John 3:16-21). When Jesus died on the cross for our sins He made a way for us to be reconciled to God. He made it *possible* to reconcile, but first we

have to make a choice to repent of the things that we have done that wrong Him, of the sins we have committed.

This leads us to a key point about reconciliation and forgiveness:

Forgiving only takes one person. Reconciliation takes two people. To be reconciled with someone there must be repentance from the wrongdoer as well as forgiveness on the part of the person wronged.

Choosing to forgive someone involves a **vertical** transaction—directly between your heart and the Father heart of God. On the other hand, **reconciliation is horizontal**; it occurs between you and another person, and *both* people must be active participants in the process. Therefore, reconciliation isn't always possible since it depends on the two addressing the issues honestly and coming back together to reestablish healthy boundaries and earn trust once more.[75]

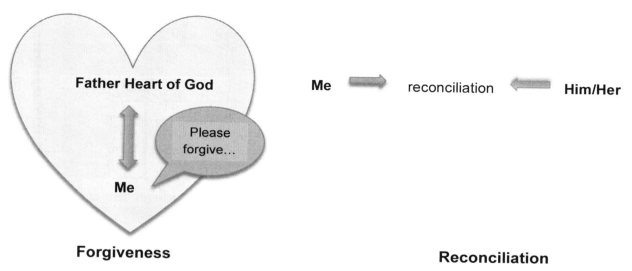

  Which of the five myths have you believed about forgiveness? How have those false beliefs affect you?

_____

_____

_____

Forgiving is . . .

Truth #1: Hard.
Jesus models what forgiveness looks like. But unlike us, He <u>NEVER</u> sinned. He physically took on the consequences of our sinful choices when He died for you and me. (He *really* understands what it is like to suffer because of others' bad choices!) He was willing to suffer and die for you and me, who did sin and would continue to sin! He died so that you and I could be forgiven. Going to the cross was excruciatingly hard and it cost Jesus everything. Forgiving is not easy; it is painful. See the following quote about how forgiveness relates to love:

Forgiveness is ferocious love dripping with freshly spilled blood. Forgiveness is a heartbreaking choice to love the sinner more than you hate the sin.[76]

❧ **How have you personally experienced God's forgiveness and ferocious love?**

_____

_____

_____

_____

Truth #2: Looking at the truth.
To forgive you must look at what was done without any denial. You must take the bandage off the gaping wound and address what is in there. Left untreated it will cause infection and illness in you. Examples of infection and illness include bitterness, low self-esteem, envy, self-hatred, resentment, vindictiveness, sarcasm, depression, anger, and hatred directed at others. These "infections" left untreated will spread like cancer, causing death to your spirit and mind if not your body.

During His last supper with His disciples, Jesus predicted that one of them would betray Him. Judas, who had already made arrangements to betray Jesus, responded to Him, *"Surely not I, Rabbi?"* Jesus answered him, *"Yes, it is you."* He told the disciples, *"This very night you will all fall away on account of me."* Then, when Peter swore that he would *never* do such a thing, Jesus gave him very specific details of how even he, Peter, would abandon Him. **Jesus *spoke truth*** to all of them about how they would betray and abandon Him. (Matthew 26)

Truth #3: A choice, not a feeling.
Christ on the cross chose to forgive when He pleaded, *"Father, forgive them, for they do not know what they're doing"* (Luke 23:34). His body was racked with pain from physical beatings He had just endured. He had heard their accusations, hate, and lies against Him. And yet He saw beyond all of that to the truth that the very people who had made all those terrible choices really did not understand the ramifications of their vicious, angry words and actions. We, too, can choose to forgive even when we are not pain-free.

Forgiving is a choice. We have to grieve and mourn our losses and work through our feelings of anger and hurt to be set free, but it starts with a choice to forgive. Choosing not to forgive keeps you stalled in that no-man's-land where you cannot have the past as you thought it was and you cannot yet embrace the future as it will be.

Forgiveness is the key to letting go of the past and being able to move on to a new future.

❧ **Think of a time when you knew you should forgive someone, but didn't feel like it. Tell about your experience.**

_____

_____

_____

_____

Truth #4: Something that starts with just you and God.

Jesus had taken three disciples to support Him and pray with Him during His greatest time of need, and yet, more than once, Jesus returned only to find them asleep. They didn't really understand what He was going through. (I believe that He really wanted their support and that is why He kept waking them up.) Yet He struggled alone, on His face, crying out to His Father in heaven. Forgiving can be very lonely. That is often the way it is for you who have experienced trauma.

No one completely understands the agonizing pain you have gone through—not your best friend, not your family, and not the person who wounded you. **When you forgive someone you are taking part in a miracle that hardly anyone notices.** No person can record this miracle on Facebook or in a digital photo because it happens in the privacy of your inner self, silently, invisibly between your heart and the heart of Father God.

Truth #5: A process.

The decision to forgive is the beginning of a process. It is simply your agreement to examine what the trauma has cost you. Like the layers of an onion, each layer of the wound will need to be looked at, grieved, and forgiven. Each layer that slips away will allow a deeper layer to show.

Peggy

The layers terrified me. How much more could there be? Would the layers never end? I felt the stench of the onion burning my eyes and the scent of it destroying my soul. Yet, one day I realized the layers were a tender expression of God's incredible love for me. He knew that I could only handle one layer at a time, that to have to deal with everything that had happened (the whole onion) all at once would destroy me. So He lovingly allowed me to see one layer at a time, when He knew I was ready to handle it. Now, when He reveals another layer to me I get excited, not about how painful and "stinky" it will be, but because I know it means He believes I am now ready and able to deal with it. Each layer has become proof that I have grown!

In Matthew 18:21-22, Peter came to Jesus and asked how many times he had to forgive when his brother sinned against him. Jesus answered him, *"Seventy times seven."* I believe Jesus was letting Peter know about the onion! Forgiveness is an ongoing process, piece-by-piece, layer-by-layer.

  ✒ **Describe a time in which you had to forgive that involved a more extended process.** Consider your initial age at the time of the event and how more truths of the event were revealed in time. Describe your own growth and development since then and the continued actions of the offender(s).

_____

_____

_____

_____

_____

Truth #6: Freedom

Forgiving allows you to be set free from the bondage and burden of bitterness and resentment. It allows you to let go of the control over yourself and others and gives that control back to God. When you have worked through the process of forgiving, you are free to be who God made you to be—open and transparent, not stuck in woundedness and the past. Forgiving literally frees you from destructive thinking.

Much of the pain you have been medicating with your compulsive behavior may have its roots in your inability to face your anger and process forgiveness towards those who have wounded you.

**The person who gains the most from forgiveness
is the person who does the forgiving.**[77]

One of the most effective tools the enemy uses to steal our joy is unforgiveness. With just a little foothold of unforgiveness in our lives, we can easily become bound with chains of bitterness, resentment, anger, and rage. If we let that foothold linger without dealing with it, eventually it will lead to our own self-destruction.

Choosing to not forgive the unrighteous actions of others and yourself can easily become a stumbling block in your path to healing. Scripture encourages all believers to have forgiving hearts (see Ephesians 4:32, Colossians 3:13, Matthew 6:12-15 and 18:21-35). It is not just for the sake of being like Christ; there is great joy in realizing that when you forgive others, you actually release yourself by becoming unchained from their hurtful actions.

∽ **From God's perspective, why do you think He wants us to have a forgiving spirit?**

_____

_____

_____

_____

∽ **What would be the biggest benefit or blessing to you personally if you could totally forgive?**

_____

_____

_____

❧ **Choose someone from your "People Who Hurt Me" list and begin the process of forgiveness by writing a letter of forgiveness.** (The person might be one to whom you wrote an anger letter at the beginning of this chapter.)

Dear _____,

This day I am choosing to forgive you for _____

_____

_____

_____

_____

_____

_____

_____

_____

_____

_____

_____

_____

_____

At some point it will be important to repeat this process with all the names on your "People Who Hurt Me" list.

❧ **After finishing your letter write a prayer, sharing with God your feelings about forgiving this person. Ask Him to seal your choice of forgiveness with a sense of His peace.**

_____

_____

_____

_____

_____

_____

_____

❧ In what areas do you need to apply God's forgiveness in your own life? What past choices have you made for which you struggle to forgive yourself?

_____

_____

_____

❧ Complete the statement: It is hard to forgive myself because . . .

_____

_____

_____

Jesus assures us in the Lord's Prayer that God will forgive us as we forgive others. John also underlines that truth and assures us of God's forgiveness:

> *If I confess **my** sins, He is faithful and just to forgive **my** sins*
> *and to cleanse **me** from all unrighteousness.*
> 1 John 1:9 (NKJ--personalized)

Listen to David's anguish as he wrestled with guilt over his sin with Bathsheba until giving way to confession:

> *When I kept silent, my bones wasted away through my groaning all day long.*
> *For day and night your hand was heavy upon me;*
> *my strength was sapped as in the heat of summer.*
>
> *Then I acknowledged my sin to you and did not cover up my iniquity.*
> *I said, "I will confess my transgressions to the LORD "—*
> *and you forgave the guilt of my sin.*
> Psalm 32:3-5 (NIV)

David understood that God allows you to feel guilt to get your attention. However, when you continue to blame yourself after being forgiven, you are keeping a record of wrongs—your own wrongs.

The ability to forgive yourself is impacted by your understanding of grace. Grace is <u>undeserved</u> favor, or getting what we don't deserve. Grace is not grace if you have to be good enough for it. Grace is accepting what you don't deserve (i.e., forgiveness). Mercy is <u>not</u> getting what you <u>do</u> deserve (i.e., punishment).

≈ **What is one thing for which you would like to be forgiven?**
Write a prayer like David's, acknowledging your sin and asking God to forgive you. Then date it. The enemy will want you to continue to pick up a whip and beat yourself over your past sins and mistakes, but each time he does you can point to the date and declare to the enemy, **"I AM FORGIVEN."**

Dear God:

_____

_____

_____

_____

_____

_____

_____

_____

Date _____

Now declare out loud: **Whom the Son sets free is free indeed.** (John 8:36)

Song recommendations for meditation this week:

Dear X (You Don't Own Me)
By Disciple

and

7 x 70
by Chris August

Assignments

1. Find a quiet space and spend 15 minutes reflecting on Angela's picture (following page).

2. Complete the next chapter.

"Release"

🔹 Write your reaction to Angela's picture titled "Release."

_____

_____

_____

_____

_____

_____

Chapter 14
Discovering Your dreams

What are your dreams and how do you make them come true?

In this season of being a grandparent (Diane), our family is often treated to some kind of performance by one or more of our four grandchildren. It is amazing how young children can create entertainment for us that includes song, dance and even Tae Kwan Do all in one performance. As I mentioned in Chapter 10, one of our granddaughters was dancing around the room and my husband asked, " Are you my little ballerina?" She turned and looked at grandpa as if he was clueless and emphatically stated, "I'm a prima ballerina!" At age seven she was dreaming of herself as the main star of a ballet company.

❧ Share some of the dreams you had as a child.

_____

_____

_____

❧ Ask your friends, a teacher, or relatives what talents they have seen in you.

_____

_____

_____

Children have the capacity to see the possibilities and to dream without limits. God places that in all of us. But sometimes our dreams and desires give way to conformity and we put on a mask, adapting ourselves to the expectations of others, real or imagined. That is where Jessica and Angela found themselves.

Jessica

I recently came face to face with my personal trauma. I understand now that I have been trapped in a box, and have been making decisions based on what other people would think of me. I visualized myself in that box and God showed me something amazing. Watching myself hunched down in self-hatred, I see my God-given wings have been squashed, stuffed down, and ignored. I have felt ashamed of being uniquely different because I was afraid of what others would think of me. Once I stopped trying to please other people, I was free to like myself for who I am. I started trusting my gut and making decisions on my own, and am discovering I am a capable woman. I understand now that I can take care of myself because I am worth it, not simply because I am trying to impress someone.

It has taken months of practice and meditating on God's truths, but my life is changing. I no longer have to stay in my box to feel accepted. I can live authentically and take responsibility for myself. I am in the process of building self-confidence and I now have authority to speak into the lives of other young women going through the same thing. Instead of being trapped in a crazy cycle of love addiction, I can finally rest in my heart. For the first time, I see that I have God-given wings to soar above other people's expectations and fly anywhere He is.

Hidden dreams I never before recognized have started to surface. I had heard about knowing God's calling for one's life, but never knew what He had for me. As I take steps of obedience towards health, I see that God is growing my dreams into a specific calling. I know that God has called me to rest and peace instead of anxiety. I know that I have a deep desire to help others heal from their past traumas. I want to adopt children who need healthy homes. I have done the hard work and I am living a life richer than I could have ever have imagined.

One painful hurt was how family members corrected my English when I was growing up. These memories triggered feelings of worthlessness and lack of acceptance as I moved into my teen and adult years. Ironically, I am now using my English skills to publish my first book about healing past wounds!

When I read Isaiah 49:11, something awakened within me. The Lord is talking to Isaiah about restoring Israel. He states, "I will turn all my mountains into roads, and my highways will be raised up." I think of the mountain of healing and know that God turns my mountains into roads and gives me great peace.

Angela

As a child, I received enormous peace through artistic drawing and writing. It was my quiet spot—the one place where the mask fell off, the labels were peeled away, and I felt alive. Through years of being raised in a loud, explosive, abusive home, those talents were set aside as I focused on running away. I didn't party a lot at that time, but spent many days in bed, rolled into a fetal position, imagining how I could end my life without pain. By the grace of God, I never could come up with a painless way to end my life.

God's grace saved me. He always sent a hug from a friend at just the right moment. As the years progressed I married and then separated from my husband. Following the stillbirth of my son Andrew, I divorced. I judged and condemned my life. I had, after all, stayed in a violent marriage. My son died and I lived. I was unworthy. But God said it was not over. He was not finished with me. Life was a struggle and God was faithful. Now I have three beautiful children.

It was in that place of being given what I felt I never deserved that the passion for artistic drawing came to life again. In the midst of poverty, trying to figure out how to bless my children as a mother, I started painting for them. First murals, then Halloween costumes, and slowly the art, like giving birth, began to come alive again. It was like drawing in your first breath. I felt indescribable joy whenever I painted or wrote. It was a place I thought I would never revisit. I had always blown my opportunities. In high school I had an abortion and I closed every door and walked away instead of pursuing good things.

Never in my wildest dreams did I imagine that God would break through the ruins and offer me life again. Words can't describe how grateful and excited I am to be able to use what God has given me to bring peace and joy to others! I can see the value of who I am, not based upon what I have done, but who He says I am. As I paint and write I find deeper healing and relationship with my best friend Jesus. When the mask drops, my heart melts before Him. As I *write or paint I find life, joy, peace, a future and a hope. He has freed me to express my heart and to worship Him. God stepped in and gave me the life I was created to live.*

Hidden Treasures

There were hidden treasures in each of these women. Sometimes these treasures are hard to see, especially if we have tried to imitate or please others rather than discover what God has hidden in us. God loves to surprise us with the hidden treasures He has deposited in His children. Look at these examples from the Bible:

- He hid a warrior inside a shepherd boy named David; even Goliath was surprised.
- He hid a deliverer of His people inside a fugitive murderer named Moses.
- He hid a queenly deliverer of His people inside an orphaned Jewish girl named Esther.
- He hid an evangelist inside the woman at the well despite her sinful reputation.
- He hid a King and Savior inside a manger.

What has God hidden inside of you?

But we have this treasure in earthen vessels that the excellence of the power may be of God and not of us.

2 Corinthians 4:7 (NKJ)

What a paradox! God can take weak human beings and use them for instruments of power in this world. God has deposited in each of us talents, treasures, and divine dreams that can be a legacy for others.

God has given you gifts in the past and present.

To understand God's future plans for you, it's important to take an inventory of your victories, talents, and gifts, both past and present.

The following exercise will help you think through what God might be saying to you about your accomplishments, your dreams, and your purpose. The first chart will help you look back at your victories, events, and friendships that have been significant to you and/or others.

> **Desires of Your Heart**
> **By Angela**

☙ **Write the answers from your life in the following chart.**

The gifts God has given me from my past and present

Past Victories	Use of talents and gift	Relationships built from these experiences
Example: Auditioned for & made the cut for Kid's choir.	Ministering with my love of music and worship in Kid's choir	In choir I met Maria, who is my best friend to this day.
Example: Joined & excelled on school debate team.	Developed my skills of speaking to an audience.	Debate team coach believed in me and encouraged my speaking gifts.
Example: Junior Counselor at kids camp.	Grew in my skills in leading and being there for kids.	Created life long relationships with other Jr. Counselors.

☙ **What patterns do you notice about your gifts, talents, experiences or relationships? What trait, talents, or unique gift might be present in you for His glory?**

Example: Creative arts seem to be a reoccurring theme and passion.

Example: I like helping the teacher at school by coming alongside others who need help. I did the same as a Junior Counselor at camp. I love teaching children.

_____

_____

_____

_____

_____

Your legacy: Gifts for others

In light of the treasures God has deposited in you, what is the legacy He wants you to give to others? Ask Him what He has in mind for the remaining years you have on this earth.

꙰ **Draw a picture of what God might have you leave for others.** (Use words, pictures, symbols, or whatever comes to mind as you listen to what God is speaking through His Holy Spirit to you.)

꙰ **Write a brief description of what you have drawn.**

_____

_____

_____

_____

_____

In order to move into those dreams and desires, we often need character changes and wisdom to inhabit those future places of blessing. This chart will help you think through how to move forward into God's dreams through building your foundation, ensuring progress and success.

The Gifts God Wants Me to Develop

Action steps I can take in the year ahead to further my life goals and character development	God's dreams for me
A. Example: Identify two trusted friends who have my same values so I can enjoy a year of sobriety & accountability.	A. I will become a healthy young woman who has made good choices to live out my Christian values.
B. Example: Find a mentor who can help me grow in areas I feel there has been a lack.	B. I will have new spiritual and relational skills to pass on to others.
1.	1.
2.	2.
3.	3.
4.	4.

  Circle one action step you want to work on in the next month. Who can you ask to keep you accountable for taking action in the next month?

_____

  Personalize and make this your prayer:

> Lord,
> Thank you for the talents, treasures, and dreams You have deposited in me. You know how I began and when my life will end; my times are in Your hands. I want to make the most of the rest of my life and, with Your help, I want to leave a legacy that glorifies You. Open my heart for all You have for me that I might experience the abundant life You have promised. May my life of love for You and surrender to Your purpose be a source of blessing and a rich legacy for my family, my friends, and my descendants.
>
> Signed: _____ Date _____

Song recommendation for meditation this week:
The Cave
by Mumford & Sons

Chapter 15
Mask-Free Living!

Looking out on the frosty morning, Jessica bundled up with her leather jacket and wrapped a wool scarf around her neck. It had become a weekly habit to treat herself to coffee one morning a week. When she got to the coffee shop, the comforting smells of freshly baked muffins and strong lattes awakened her senses. She sat at her favorite table and glanced through the window that overlooked the sunrise. Jessica pulled out her Bible and journal and prayed that God would give her the strength to be herself today. Taking a sip of warm coffee and then placing a pen in her hand, she wrote a poem about the new life into which she was venturing.

> *In my mind, I am sitting in that field of grass. Jesus, I know you are near.*
> *You have opened my eyes, removed my mask, and revealed to me the pain I endured.*
> *I see my wounds, I'm aware of my scars; I do not need to hide what You can see.*
> *I cared for myself less than You care for me.*
> *I grieve what was lost, say goodbye to the past.*
> *I accept what you have for me, a new life without a mask.*
> *Now, I walk forward, with You by my side.*
> *I no longer have anything to hide.*

Jessica, Anna and Cindy are real women who have done the same difficult work that you have done by walking through this book. Anna is applying to colleges and daily working on valuing herself and standing strong with what she has learned. Cindy is a successful businesswoman who leads a girls' group and helps others trust in God to heal them as she has been healed. After years of processing her trauma, Cindy is now at a place where she can practice healthy boundaries in relationships and find validation in Christ rather than in men. Jessica is also leading a young women's group and is learning how to care for and value herself every day. Her relationships become more authentic as she understands that she is a strong and distinct person from those around her. Like them, your journey isn't over.

If you have honestly finished this work, you are well on your way to seeing growth in your life and in the lives around you. We hope that you have identified unhealthy patterns in your life, discovered the root underneath, and now have tools to help you live an authentic life, free of sexual immorality and full of genuine, God-given intimacy. In times of stress will you feel pressured to put your masks back on? Probably! But it is for those times you have a mentor, a plan and/or accountability people. Remember that Jessica, Anna, and Cindy have all seen their lives completely change as they practice what they have learned and stay accountable to individuals or a group such as a *Behind the Mask* group.

The last chapter of this book does not mean the end of a journey, but rather the beginning of approaching life in a new way. We recognize the work you have done so far has been important and difficult work. Sometimes it may have seemed impossible. You may still feel haunted by the masks of your past. But you are making new pathways in your brain, creating new habit patterns. Understanding the principles in this chapter will help you continue your forward momentum.

Each of us is unique; that means God works with each of us in different ways. He had Abraham take a walk (to the promised land), Elijah take a nap (after running from his enemy), and Joshua take a lap (around the walls of Jericho). Jesus was stern with the rich young ruler, tender with the woman caught in adultery, and gracious with the thief on the Cross.

> **How has God been uniquely working in your life as you have walked through this book?**

_____

_____

_____

_____

As unique as each of our journeys are, the following parable presents a powerful picture of the results when we ask God to work in our lives.

> *Then he told this parable: "A man had a fig tree growing in his vineyard, and he went to look for fruit on it but did not find any. So he said to the man who took care of the vineyard, 'For three years now I've been coming to look for fruit on this fig tree and haven't found any. Cut it down! Why should it use up the soil?'*
>
> *"'Sir,' the man replied, 'leave it alone for one more year, and I'll dig around it and fertilize it. If it bears fruit next year, fine! If not, then cut it down.'"*
> Luke 13:6-9 (NIV)

Notice the initial condition of the tree: there was a lack of fruit and a negative evaluation. When you first started your journey, the pull of peer pressure and worldly choices may have caused you to feel like that barren tree, with little or no Christ-like fruit in your life.[78]

Let's look at four steps that allow a life to bear much fruit.

Step 1: Remove yourself from judgment.

Unlike the owner of the vineyard, God fortunately doesn't say, "Cut it down. Why should it use up the soil?" The vineyard caretaker steps before the judge and declares, "Wait a minute, hold off on that negative judgment." And who is that judge? It isn't God, the cross settled that. The judge is the critical voice most of us have whispering in our head. It is the voice that can keep us stuck in our past. Nothing grows under judgment. Judgment can only render a verdict and a sentence. It can never change someone.

God's desire is for us to grow and move to a new destination—much like the GPS we have in our car to help us find our travel destination. The voice on my GPS is a female with a British accent; somehow she seems quite smart and I have confidence that she knows which path of travel is best. The great thing is, she doesn't shame me when I take a wrong turn. She doesn't say, "You idiot, you made a wrong turn. You never get it right. You think I am going to help you now? You can just find your own way!" Instead she says, "When safe to do so, execute a U turn."

The critical step to real change is realizing the source of the negative voices and lies. As you spent time processing your trauma, you discovered that God's Truth about you counters those lies.

> **In contrast to lies that pop up in your mind, who does God say you are?**

_____

_____

Step 2: Allow God to deal with the root structure of your soul.

In previous chapters you let Him dig deep below the surface of your masks and began to discover the pain that was driving much of your unwanted behavior. You identified wounds and fears, times of rejection and abandonment, and grieved your losses. You began to realize you needed to feel those painful things in order to heal and change. For some of you the root structure from other trees (family members, boyfriends, girlfriends, etc.) were choking your roots with their toxic or hurtful statements.

> **Looking back over the work you have done and the things you discovered, what impacted your root system the most?**

_____

_____

_____

Step 3: Bring outside resources into your life.

The caretaker of the vineyard goes on to say that the tree needs to be fertilized. Nutrients and outside resources need to be brought in for the tree to produce fruit. There are a number of outside resources you can bring into your life in order to produce a lifestyle that reflects a growing Christ-likeness.

Accountability
Seek on-going accountability in a group or another relationship where someone knows all your stuff and loves you anyway, and who also will challenge you to make good decisions.

> **Name one or two people who you can ask to hold you accountable to the goals you set for yourself. When will you talk to these people?**

_____

Self-Care: Creating healthy structures in your life
Developing a long-term self-care plan may be a challenge for many. Indeed, many young women realize they have been neglecting themselves. Changing the focus on personal care may seem strange and almost selfish. However, _there is only one you_ and only you can keep yourself healthy and growing. Becoming more in touch with your needs, hopes, and dreams throughout this journey will help you develop a healthy lifestyle.

➣ **As you work on developing your long-term care plan, you are encouraged to consider the following ideas. Check the ones that you want to become a part of your daily routine.**

❏ Deep breathing and meditation/worship to increase oxygen levels in the brain and become better in tune with yourself and centered on Christ.

❏ Surround yourself with hope-filled messages through the books you read, music you hear, media you enjoy, and friends and groups with which you interact.

❏ Regular exercise to increase blood flow and body strength, as well as to release muscle tension.

❏ Regular interaction with healthy Christian friends for problem-solving, validation, encouragement, and prayer.

❏ Create new healthy rituals to nurture yourself, utilizing your restoration needs as indicated by the FASTER scale.

❏ Incorporate more creative/right-brained activities into daily life for greater joy and health (such as singing, fine arts, dance, crafts, music, writing).

❏ Journal regularly to increase your connection with God and yourself.

❏ When you feel stuck, use the Double Bind exercise to look at options, solve problems, and avoid obsession.

❏ Get good sleep to rejuvenate and heal the body and brain.

❏ Avoid toxic substances (such as drugs, cigarettes, excessive alcohol, caffeine, fast-food) and toxic attitudes (such as bitterness, rage, unforgiveness, pride, hopelessness, helplessness).

❏ Obtain counseling to work through trauma issues.

❏ Take this class again as a refresher or be a co-leader to help more of your friends come to health.

Who will hold you accountable to begin and continue one or more items you checked on this list?

_____

Step 4: Become a Safe Person

As you daily choose to practice healthier living, two essential elements will help you become a safe person for yourself and others. The book *Safe People* describes those two important characteristics: (1) healthy boundaries and (2) having the ability to be self-assertive.[79]

The following characteristics of safe and unsafe people will help you recognize authenticity in yourself and those you date.[80]

Safe People	Unsafe People
Admit their weaknesses	Think they "have it all together"
Are spiritual	Are religious
Are open to feedback	Are defensive
Are humble	Are self-righteous
Apologize and change behavior	Only apologize
Deal with their problems	Avoid working on their problems
Earn trust	Demand trust
Admit their faults	Believe they are perfect
Take responsibility	Blame others
Tell the truth	Lie
Are growing	Are stagnant

The characteristics listed under unsafe people should remind you of some of the masks you identified in the first chapter of this book.

❧ **Which characteristics will you begin to work on?**

_____

When you become the safe, authentic person Christ created you to be, others around you will feel safe enough to risk shedding their masks. You will be giving them the gift, the freedom to share what is really true about them without the fear of what others will think. One person—you—can make a difference in the lives of others by courageously modeling authenticity.

❧ **Who will hold you accountable to work on one or two of these characteristics, thus becoming a safe person?**

_____

Once you start understanding what "healthy" looks like as an individual, it is important to take your healthy perspective to a new level.

What will a healthy marriage look like?
JRR Tolkien penned a classic statement amidst a poignant scene in his _Lord of the Rings_ books. It had become clear that someone noble had to return the all-powerful Ring to the dreaded Land of Mordor to put an end to Sauron's evil attacks. Finally, the brave Frodo Baggins steps forward hesitantly offering, "I will take the Ring, though I do not know the way."[81]

No couple "knows the way" as they embark on the journey called marriage. But the Bible does tell us not to be unequally yoked, which means a Christian and non-believer in any dating relationship that could lead to marriage. I have counseled more women who thought they could witness to their boyfriend-now husband and bring him to the Lord. With tears in their eyes they say, "Our intimacy level has never grown because we have so little in common."

- He doesn't have the same friends—because he is not a Christian.
- He thinks going out drinking with the guys regularly is OK—because he is not a Christian.
- He won't go to church with me—because he is not a Christian.
- He wants to raise our children differently—because he is not a Christian.

- He doesn't share my values—because he is not a Christian.
- He wants me to join with him in watching porn—because he is not a Christian.

The list goes on and on. God doesn't warn, "Don't be unequally yoked" because He is mean. He knows the deepest needs and desires of a Christian woman can only be filled if together the husband and wife are walking down the same path, with Christ as the center of their relationship.

Only those sharing Christian values can fully experience healthy sex. The chart that follows shows you the values that lead to intimacy and closeness versus unhealthy sex that destroys intimacy.

Healthy Sexuality	Unhealthy Sexuality
Is respectful	Degrades & shames
Fun & exciting	Demanding & obligatory
Is victimless	Victimizes & exploits
Is intimate	Lacks emotional attachment
Mutuality in needs expressed	Needs dominated by one
Trust is foundational	Built on dishonesty
Is safe	Is unsafe, creating fear
Serves to connect emotionally	Serves to medicate pain
Creates warmth & oneness	Meets self-focused needs
Deepens values & beliefs	Compromises values & beliefs
Is authentic	Reflects a double-life

1 Corinthians 13:4-6 (MSG) defines biblical love—the attitude and behavior of any Christian toward another person. When the relationship involves dating or marriage, can you also see how this describes the attributes necessary for healthy sexuality?

> ....Love cares more for others than for self.
> Love doesn't want what it doesn't have.
> ....Doesn't force itself on others,
> Isn't always "me first,"
> Doesn't fly off the handle,
> ....Takes pleasure in the flowering of truth,
> Always looks for the best....

Authentic intimacy that reflects 1 Corinthians 13 and embraces the value of being equally yoked can be described this way:

Real intimacy is relating rightly to another person (and God) with honesty, transparency, caring, acceptance and commitment. True intimacy is a by-product of my shared life with Christ and a transparent life with my husband.[82]

∽ **Write a prayer expressing to God the qualities you want in your future mate.**

_____

_____

_____

_____

_____

_____

_____

_____

_____

_____

Premarital counseling before marriage

Premarital counseling, with the help of a Taylor-Johnson Temperament Analysis,[83] can greatly predict where some rough places might show up in your life together. When a couple gets resources before marriage to heal individually, they can look forward to a healthier marriage. Remember! Outside resources can help create good fruit.

Step 5: Give it a year.

Although you have begun to take all the previous steps—removing judgment and allowing grace to be the motivator, digging around the roots of the past, and bringing in external resources—that is not enough. The key element in the parable is realizing that healing is not instant; it is a process that takes time. You are creating new pathways in your brain. Therefore, it is important to prepare to walk out all that you have learned over time so that real fruit has a chance to grow.

∽ **What would help you to walk this out over time?**

_____

_____

_____

- **Pursue your dreams and passions**

Remember that God has uniquely created you with dreams and talents. If those are not pursued, they become stagnant and little or no fruit will grow. Commit to a periodic review of Chapter 14 where you listed the gifts and legacy you want to give others. Taking an inventory every six months and making adjustments as needed will not only help you reach your target, but will also lead to a fruitful life.

∽ **Who can keep you accountable to evaluating your goals twice a year?** _____

- **Create a Personal Treasure Trove**

A Treasure Trove is a collection of objects and treasured items that represent your journey through _Behind the Mask_. These reminders will help you withstand the onslaught of temptation you will face as you choose to walk in health. You may want to use a decorated box, a purse, a tote or a makeup bag to keep the contents together. Be creative! The contents of your treasure trove will be unique to you. Here are some suggestions you might want to consider:

- ❑ Reminders of your progress in the healing journey. Things like pictures, note cards from a group member or leader, jewelry, or any reminders of significant moments in your walk through *Behind the Mask*.
- ❑ Pictures of your *Behind the Mask* Group that remind you of positive memories.
- ❑ Pictures of friends you respect and enjoy.
- ❑ Copies of your dating plan or specific pages of this book that helped you.
- ❑ A copy of one of the pictures in this book that spoke to your heart.
- ❑ Words to one of the songs you listened to during your journey through this book.
- ❑ Favorite Scripture verses and the promises God has given you concerning your life and future.
- ❑ Phone numbers of your group members and friends to call for encouragement.
- ❑ MP3 files or the lyrics of Christian songs that God has used to touch your heart.
- ❑ The letter you are about to personalize in the next exercise.

Keep your Treasure Trove in a location where you can get to it when you need encouragement and are battling hell. If you find yourself going back to old behaviors, don't try to tough it out and try harder. Instead, pull out the treasures immediately and rehearse what the articles in it mean to you. (You will also want to quickly connect with your accountability partner or mentor.)

Personalized Letter
Telling yourself the truth with encouraging words when your survival brain wants to take over is an important strategy. Write a letter to yourself that you can read when you feel overwhelmed and are tempted to return to old lies and behaviors. The enemy will work hard to tempt you where there were former weaknesses. When you become vulnerable, what would you tell yourself to help you return to sanity?

Write out the letter in detail. At your next *Behind the Mask* meeting, have your teammates write supportive or encouraging comments on sticky notes and attach them to your letter. This letter will go in your Personal Treasure Trove. You may want to write a summary of your letter on a 3 X 5 card and carry it with you at all times.

Your letter should address the following:
- What emotions and issues would lead you to read this letter? (When I feel lonely, rejected, abandoned, worthless, peer pressure from a boyfriend, etc.)
- What will happen if you ignore the good things God has done in you?
- What must you do to avoid going back to old ways of thinking and behaviors?
- What's the God-given dream you have in your soul?
- What truths and encouraging words do you need to hear at this moment?
- What has God said about you?
- What tools did you gain to fight the battle for purity? How can you implement them right now?

Here is an example of one young woman's letter to herself:

Dear Cindy,

You are probably reading this letter because you are facing some difficult and overwhelming situations. But just because you are struggling doesn't mean you have to give in. It feels overwhelming right now because you're probably alone and want to feel better fast.

You are probably facing a double bind right now: "Do I return to old behaviors from my past for a moment of pleasure or do I face the pain I am feeling and ask for God and others to help me through?" Remember, the right thing is the hard thing.

Cindy, also remember you have traveled this path many times before. You made decisions you deeply regretted and felt loaded down by shame. Also, remember you will have to put on a mask and hide what you did from others and lie about it. What you think is a quick fix will always make you feel more empty and lonely. You'll feel sorrow over your broken commitments to God and others, especially your small group members. And most of all, your God-given dreams will become soiled and seem impossible.

Cindy, hell is whispering false promises into your soul, promises that never work. So identify where the pain is and what you need.

> *If you're lonely or bored ....call a friend.*
> *If you're feeling worthless............rehearse what God says about you.*
> *If you're angry or overwhelmed...share your feelings with God or a friend.*
> *If you're hungry or tired..............eat something healthy or rest.*

If your friends, your parents, or a member of your Behind the Mask *group could see what you are about to do, would you still do it? Remember you are called of God and set apart for His purposes. He designed your life to make a difference.*

Remember you matter to Christ. You are the apple of His eye and He wants to continue the good work He has begun in you. Rehearse what God has said and promised to you, and call a friend and share those things with her right now.

> *Love ya,*
> *Cindy*

– **Write a personal letter to yourself right now.**

As you follow the steps outlined in this chapter for mask-free living, you will be creating healthy habits that will transform you over time into the woman God had in mind when He created you. God can enter new places of your heart and use your natural talents for supernatural purposes as you become intentional about removing the masks and redirecting the pathways in your brain. Your calling can become clear. Your purpose becomes eternal. The real "you" comes forth in full radiance and beauty.

– **Bring your Treasure Trove, including your letter, to your next *Behind the Mask* group. Maybe your group wants to plan a time of celebration and rejoicing that includes sharing some of the items each person selected for her Treasure Trove.**

Song recommendation for meditation this week:
Open Wide
By Future of Forestry

Most Frequently Asked Questions

With responses by Ted & Diane Roberts

Questions young adult women most frequently ask

Is oral sex outside of marriage immoral?
Since 50% of 15 to 18 year olds have experienced oral sex, it is to be expected that there would be a large number of questions about this behavior. Oral sex is sex, and any sex outside of marriage is not appropriate from God's perspective. God says to flee sexual immorality and makes marriage the boundary for all sexual contact. (1 Thessalonians 4; 1 Corinthians 6) The first question to ask about any sexual behavior outside of marriage: Does it raise sexual expectations that cannot righteously be fulfilled? Genital contact between unmarried people definitely raises sexually inappropriate expectations. Oral sex also puts you in danger of contracting an STD (sexually transmitted disease). With any genital contact, STD's can be spread.

Can you get life-threatening sexually transmitted diseases just through kissing?
Some diseases can be transmitted through kissing if a person is carrying certain STD's. They are more often then not transmitted through genital contact, which includes oral sex.

If you both have never had sex and it is your first time, can you still get an STD?
It depends on what you mean by "you never have had sex." If there has been any genital contact by either person, there is a possibility of one person having an STD without knowing it.

What about self-stimulation (masturbation)?
Self-stimulation creates a self-focus that can change your brain. If it becomes habitual, future intimacy with a marriage partner will become impossible because your mind has been trained to focus on fantasy and your own needs, rather than being present and meeting the needs of your spouse.

Can pornographic music affect me?
I (Diane) have counseled a number of gals who say that suggestive (pornographic) music is part of their ritual of acting out sexually. Polluting your mind creates highways in the brain that lead you in the opposite direction that God has for you, both spiritually and sexually.

Can I get my virginity back?
Sadly, no. But you can decide to make a new commitment to purity from this point on, and I encourage you do that with other girls in a *Behind the Mask* group. With the help of that group, you will be able to say to your future spouse, "I am sorry for the choices I made before I joined an accountability group, but from that point on, I received healing, real accountability, and tools to walk in purity so I could save myself for you."

How can I deal with desires to have sex before marriage?
I would encourage you to join a *Behind the Mask* group or another group that creates a band of sisters who support each other in walking in sexual purity. There is something powerful that happens when sisters in the Lord support you in your efforts to delay sex until marriage.

How far is too far before marriage?
Here's a simple definition of premarital boundaries: Anything from the neck down is off limits!

If there is no sex before marriage, how can I make sex go smoothly without any awkward moments on my wedding night?
You can't. Part of true, growing intimacy in a marriage is that you will often feel uncomfortable in being close. Learning to love each other is a lifetime mission.

Is it OK to have sex when you are married, just for fun without trying to have a child?
Absolutely! God created sex so that we might enjoy it. Here is a quote from the *Sexy Christians* book: "…the clitoris has nine thousand nerve endings, but none of those are required for the act of procreation any more than the taste buds in our mouth are required for the act of eating. This fact underlines the good news that God created our taste buds and nerve endings for pure pleasure."

How can I be closer to God if I am always judged for being Gay Girl?
First, I encourage you to complete the chapters and do all the exercises in *Behind the Mask*. At one point, the same sex attraction is addressed. Many young women, out of their hurt and fear of men, think same sex attraction is natural, when in reality it is masking the hurt of their past. God wants you to understand who He has created you to be without the trappings of society's labels and conclusions. If wounds of your past are not addressed, you will make assumptions that lead to wrong conclusions. Same sex acting out is trying to meet a legitimate need in an illegitimate way.

How does sex outside of marriage affect my relationship with God?
You can't ignore what God has to say and have a good relationship with Him. God's desire is to help you integrate every area of your life to glorify Him, including the area of your sexuality. Any sexual activity outside of marriage creates an illusion that you can be a Christian publicly but ignore His guidelines in private. Such choices cause you to compartmentalize your spiritual and sexual behavior. This not only creates a facade of wearing masks to hide your behavior, but also causes you to miss the deep spiritual implications of the sexual relationship God created for you to enjoy. Abiding in God's truths will allow you to walk down the road of blessing. Choosing to go down your own path will hurt you and create a lot of pain.

Questions young adult guys most frequently ask

The number one question by far is the issue of oral sex.
Since 50% of 15 to 18 year olds have experienced oral sex, it is to be expected that there would be a large number of questions about this behavior. The first question to ask about any sexual behavior outside of marriage is: Does it raise sexual expectations that cannot righteously be fulfilled? Oral sex is sex, and any sex outside of marriage is not appropriate from God's perspective. Genital contact between two unmarried people is definitely raising sexually inappropriate expectations. Oral sex also puts you in danger of contracting an STD (sexually transmitted disease).

What is wrong with masturbation?
While it is not the unpardonable sin, if it becomes a habit it can be deadly. When you masturbate there is no release of "prolactin" in your brain, which means there is not a deep

sense of fulfillment like you will have sex with your future mate. Therefore, masturbation will trigger you to constantly seek more. As it becomes a habit, you eventually will become a terrible lover for your future spouse because you will always be looking for a "quick fix." Women are not as quickly excited sexually as men; they take awhile to get up to speed. When you add porn to a masturbation habit, the results can become particularly deadly. For the first time in history, teen guys are reporting erectile dysfunction. Their addiction to porn and masturbation is totally crippling their ability to be sexually functional.

Are wet dreams a sin?
No, they are a natural part of the process of sexual maturation.

What are the steps to help you stop watching porn?
One simple preventative step is accountability software, such as Covenant Eyes, on all your Internet accessing electronic devices. Be aware that porn doesn't just exist on the Internet; it can appear everywhere around you. If you have viewed porn more than a couple times, it has changed your brain. Therefore, it is almost impossible to stop your behavior on your own. Guys need to get together with a bunch of guys and walk through the *Top Gun* workbook and help each other get free.

How do you rewire your brain?
Coming out of a bondage to masturbation and/or porn is not a process you can pull off alone. Loneliness is part of what drives the addiction. You need to get together with other guys and do *Top Gun* together. Make sure you do all the exercises, not just skim through the workbook. If you faithfully do the exercises with the help of a team of other young men, you can truly experience the joy of a renewed mind!

How do I know a girl is the "right" person?
The first and most critical indicator is her walk with Christ and her sexual boundaries. If she says she loves Christ but can't keep her pants on, she is not the right girl! Secondly, friendship is a critical foundation for lasting marriage. If you can laugh together and really enjoy just talking and hanging out, that is a good indicator she may be the right one. Finally, get some quality premarital counseling before you make a total commitment.

Why are teens so sexually tempted in our day and age?
One hundred years ago people married by the time they reached their late teens. Today, most young adults probably will not get married until their late twenties. In our sex-crazed world, this is a long time to resist sex if you are trying to stay pure as you follow Christ. The world around you floods you with sexual messages from the time you are a little child. By the time you are a teen you are tempted deeply and constantly. Because of the cultural pressures around you, you will never win this battle alone; you will need a team of guys to help you walk in purity. You need a band of brothers!

Behind the Mask:
Authentic Living For Young Women

Resources

Who I Am In Christ[84]

The Word of God says:

1. **I am God's child** for I am born again of the incorruptible seed of the Word of God that lives and abides forever. (1 Peter 1:23)
2. **I am forgiven** of all my sins and washed in the blood. (Ephesians 1:7; Hebrews 9:14; Colossians 1:14; 1 John 2:12; 1 John 1:9)
3. **I am a new creation**. (2 Corinthians 5:17)
4. **I am a temple where the Holy Spirit lives**. (1 Corinthians 6:19)
5. **I am holy and without blame** before God. (Ephesians 1:4)
6. **I have been brought closer to God** through the blood of Christ. (Ephesians 2:13)
7. **I am victorious**. (Revelation 21:7)
8. **I am set free**. (John 8:31-32)
9. **I am strong** in the Lord. (Ephesians 6:10)
10. **I am more than a conqueror**. (Romans 8:37)
11. **I am sealed** with the Holy Spirit of promise. (Ephesians 1:13)
12. **I am accepted** in Jesus Christ. (Ephesians 1:5-6)
13. **I am complete** in Him. (Colossians 2:10)
14. **I am alive** with Christ. (Ephesians 2:4-5)
15. **I am free** from condemnation. (Romans 8:1)
16. **I am reconciled** to God. (2 Corinthians 5:18)
17. **I am qualified** to share in his inheritance. (Colossians 1:12)
18. **I am firmly rooted**, established in my faith and overflowing with gratefulness and thankfulness. (Colossians 2:7)
19. **I am chosen**. (1 Thessalonians 1:4; Ephesians 1:4; 1 Peter 2:9)
20. **I am an ambassador** of Christ. (2 Corinthians 5:20)
21. **I am God's workmanship** created in Christ Jesus for good works. (Ephesians 2:10)
22. **I am the apple of my Father's eye**. (Deuteronomy 32:10; Psalm 17:8)
23. **I am being changed** into his image. (2 Corinthians 3:18; Philippians 1:6)
24. **I am beloved** of God. (Colossians 3:12; Romans 1:7; 1 Thessalonians 1:4)
25. **I have obtained an inheritance**. (Ephesians 1:11)
26. **I have access** by one Spirit to the Father. (Ephesians 2:18)
27. **I have everlasting life** and will not be condemned. (John 5:24; John 6:47)
28. **I have received power**—the power of the Holy Spirit; power to lay hands on the sick and see them recover; power to cast out demons; power over all the power of the enemy; nothing shall by any means hurt me. (Mark 16:17-18; Luke 10:17-19)
29. **I can do all things** (everything) in and through Christ Jesus. (Philippians 4:13)
30. **I possess the Great One in me** because greater is He who is in me than he who is in the world. (1 John 4:4)
31. **My life is hidden with Christ** in God. (Colossians 3:3)

Feelings/Emotions
an alphabetical list of some words to express emotion & feeling

abandoned	confused	fawning	intimidated	petrified	stuffed
adequate	conspicuous	fearful	isolated	pleasant	stunned
adamant	contented	flustered	jealous	pleased	suffering
affectionate	contrite	foolish	joyous	precarious	sure
agitated	crazy	frantic	judgmental	pressured	sympathetic
agony	crushed	free	jumpy	pretty	talkative
ambivalent	deceitful	frenzied	kind	prim	teary
angry	defeated	frightened	laconic	proud	tempted
annoyed	delighted	frustrated	lazy	quarrelsome	tenacious
anxious	depleted	generous	left out	rage	tense
apathetic	desirous	glad	liberated	refreshed	tentative
astounded	despair	good	lonely	rejected	tenuous
awed	destructive	grateful	longing	relaxed	terrible
awkward	determined	gratified	lost	relieved	terrified
beautiful	different	greedy	lovely	remorse	threatened
betrayed	diffident	grief	loving	restless	thwarted
bitter	diminished	guilty	low	reverent	tired
blissful	discontented	gullible	lustful	rewarded	trapped
bold	disgusted	happy	mad	righteous	troubled
bored	distracted	harassed	mean	sad	trusting
bothered	distraught	hate	melancholy	satisfied	ugly
burdened	disturbed	helpful	miserable	scared	uneasy
calm	divided	helpless	naive	screwed up	unimportant
capable	dominated	high	naughty	self-righteous	unsettled
captivated	dubious	homesick	neglected	servile	violent
challenged	eager	honored	nervous	settled	vital
charmed	ecstatic	hopeful	nice	sexy	vivacious
cheated	electrified	horrible	nutty	shocked	vulnerable
cheerful	empty	hurt	obnoxious	silly	weary
cherished	enchanted	hysterical	obsessed	skeptical	weepy
childish	energetic	ignorant	odd	small	wholesome
childlike	enjoyment	ignored	opposed	sneaky	wicked
clever	enraptured	immoral	outraged	solemn	wonderful
combative	envious	imposed	overwhelmed	sorrowful	worried
competent	exasperated	upon	pain	spiteful	zany
competitive	excited	impressed	panicked	startled	zestful
compulsive	exhausted	infuriated	peaceful	stingy	
condemned	fascinated	inspired	persecuted		

PTSI (Post Traumatic Stress Index)[85]

The following statements typify reactions trauma victims often have to child abuse.

- Please check those that you believe apply to you.
- Although the statements are written in the present tense, if the statements have _ever_ applied in your life then place a check next to that item.
- Statements are considered false only if they have _never_ been a part of your life. If in doubt, let your first reaction be your guide.
- Given these guidelines, check the statements you feel apply to you.

PTSI

_____ 1. I have recurring memories of painful experiences.
_____ 2. I am unable to stop a childhood pattern harmful to myself.
_____ 3. I sometimes obsess about people who have hurt me and are now gone.
_____ 4. I feel bad at times about myself because of shameful experiences I believe were my fault.
_____ 5. I am a risk taker.
_____ 6. At times I have difficulty staying awake.
_____ 7. I sometimes feel separate from my body as a reaction to a flashback or memory.
_____ 8. I deny myself basic needs at times like groceries, shoes, books, medical care, rent and heat.
_____ 9. I have distressing dreams about experiences.
_____ 10. I repeat painful experiences over and over.
_____ 11. I try to be understood by those who are incapable or don't care for me.
_____ 12. I have suicidal thoughts.
_____ 13. I engage in high-risk behaviors.
_____ 14. I eat excessively to avoid problems.
_____ 15. I avoid thoughts or feelings associated with my trauma experiences.
_____ 16. I skip vacations because of lack of time or money.
_____ 17. I have periods of sleeplessness.
_____ 18. I try to recreate an early trauma experience.
_____ 19. I keep secrets from people who have hurt me.
_____ 20. I have attempted suicide.
_____ 21. I am sexual when frightened.
_____ 22. I drink to excess when life is too hard.
_____ 23. I avoid stories, parts of movies, or reminders of early painful experiences.
_____ 24. I avoid sexual pleasure.
_____ 25. I sometimes feel like an old painful experience is happening now.
_____ 26. There is something destructive I do over and over from my early life.
_____ 27. I stay in conflict with someone when I could have walked away.
_____ 28. I have suicidal thoughts.
_____ 29. I often feel sexual when I am lonely.
_____ 30. I use depressant drugs as a way to cope.
_____ 31. I am unable to recall important details of painful experiences.
_____ 32. I avoid doing "normal" activities because of fears I have.
_____ 33. I have sudden, vivid or distracting memories of painful experiences.
_____ 34. I attempt to stop activities I know are not helpful.
_____ 35. I go "overboard" to help people who have been destructive.
_____ 36. I often feel lonely and estranged from others because of painful experiences I have had.

_____ 37. I feel intensely sexual when violence occurs.
_____ 38. My procrastinating interferes with my life activities.
_____ 39. I sometimes withdraw or have lack of interest in important activities because of childhood experiences.
_____ 40. I will hoard money and not spend money on legitimate needs.
_____ 41. I am upset when there are reminders of abusive experiences like anniversaries, places or symbols.
_____ 42. I compulsively do things to others that were done to me as a young person.
_____ 43. I sometimes help those who continue to harm me.
_____ 44. I feel unable to experience certain emotions (love, happiness, sadness, etc.)
_____ 45. I feel sexual when degraded or used.
_____ 46. Sleep is a way for me to avoid life's problems.
_____ 47. I have difficulty concentrating.
_____ 48. I have attempted diets repeatedly.
_____ 49. I have difficulty sleeping.
_____ 50. My relationships are the same story over and over.
_____ 51. I feel loyal to people even though they have betrayed me.
_____ 52. I have a dim outlook on my future.
_____ 53. I feel sexual when someone is "nice" to me.
_____ 54. At times I am preoccupied with food and eating.
_____ 55. I experience confusion often.
_____ 56. I refuse to buy things even when I need them and have the money.
_____ 57. I have difficulty feeling sexual.
_____ 58. I know that something destructive I do repeats a childhood event.
_____ 59. I remain a "team" member when obviously things are becoming destructive.
_____ 60. I feel as if I must avoid depending on people.
_____ 61. I sometimes feel bad because I enjoyed experiences that were exploitive of me.
_____ 62. I abuse alcohol often.
_____ 63. I tend to be accident prone.
_____ 64. I spend much time performing "underachieving" jobs.
_____ 65. Sometimes I have outbursts of anger or irritability.
_____ 66. I do things to others that were done to me in my family.
_____ 67. I make repeated efforts to convince people who were destructive to me and not willing to listen.
_____ 68. I engage in self-destructive behaviors.
_____ 69. I get "high" on activities that were dangerous to me.
_____ 70. I use TV, reading, and hobbies as a way to numb out.
_____ 71. I go into a "fantasy" world when things are tough.
_____ 72. I am "underemployed."
_____ 73. I am extremely cautious of my surroundings.
_____ 74. I have thoughts and behaviors repeatedly that do not feel good to me.
_____ 75. I attempt to be liked by people who clearly were exploiting me.
_____ 76. I engage in self-mutilating behaviors (cutting self, burning, bruising, etc.)
_____ 77. I use drugs like cocaine or amphetamines to speed things up.
_____ 78. I have a problem with "putting off" certain tasks.
_____ 79. I use "romance" as a way to avoid problems.
_____ 80. I feel very guilty about any sexual activity.
_____ 81. I often feel that people are out to take advantage of me.

_____ 82. I revert to doing things I did as a child.
_____ 83. I am attracted to untrustworthy people.
_____ 84. I endure physical or emotional pain most people would not accept.
_____ 85. I like living on the "edge" of danger or excitement.
_____ 86. When things are difficult, I will sometimes "binge."
_____ 87. I have a tendency to be preoccupied with something else than what I need to be.
_____ 88. I have a low interest in sexual activity.
_____ 89. I am distrustful of others.
_____ 90. Some of my recurring behavior comes from early life experiences.
_____ 91. I trust people who are proven unreliable.
_____ 92. I try to be perfect.
_____ 93. I am orgasmic when hurt or beaten.
_____ 94. I use drugs to escape.
_____ 95. I use marijuana or psychedelics to hallucinate.
_____ 96. I sometimes spoil success opportunities.
_____ 97. I am startled more easily than others.
_____ 98. I am preoccupied with children of a certain age.
_____ 99. I seek people who I know will cause me pain.
_____ 100. I avoid mistakes at any cost.
_____ 101. I love to "gamble" on outcomes.
_____ 102. I work too hard so I won't have to feel.
_____ 103. I will often lose myself in fantasies rather than deal with real life.
_____ 104. I go "without" necessities for periods of time.
_____ 105. I get physical reactions to reminders of abuse experiences (breaking out in cold sweat, trouble breathing, etc.)
_____ 106. I engage in abusive relationships repeatedly.
_____ 107. I have difficulty retreating from unhealthy relationships.
_____ 108. I sometimes want to hurt myself physically.
_____ 109. I need lots of stimulation so I will not be bored.
_____ 110. I get "lost" in my work.
_____ 111. I live a "double life."
_____ 112. I vomit food or use diuretics to avoid weight gain.
_____ 113. I feel anxious about being sexual.
_____ 114. There is a certain age of children or adolescents that are sexually attractive to me.
_____ 115. I continue contact with a person who has abused me.
_____ 116. I often feel unworthy, unlovable, immoral, or sinful because of experiences I have had.
_____ 117. I like sex when it is dangerous.
_____ 118. I try to "slow down" my mind.
_____ 119. I have a life of "compartments" that others do not know about.
_____ 120. I experience periods of no interest in eating.
_____ 121. I am scared about sex.
_____ 122. There are activities that I have trouble stopping even though they are useless or destructive.
_____ 123. I am in emotional fights (divorces, lawsuits) that seem endless.
_____ 124. I often feel I should be punished for past behavior.
_____ 125. I do sexual things that are risky.
_____ 126. When I am anxious, I will do things to stop my feelings.
_____ 127. I have a fantasy life that I retreat to when things are hard.

_____ 128. I have difficulty with play.
_____ 129. I wake up with upsetting dreams.
_____ 130. My relationships seem to have the same dysfunctional pattern.
_____ 131. There are certain people who I always allow to take advantage of me.
_____ 132. I have a sense that others are always better off than me.
_____ 133. I use cocaine or amphetamines to heighten "high risk" activities.
_____ 134. I don't tolerate uncomfortable feelings.
_____ 135. I am a daydreamer.
_____ 136. At times, I see comfort, luxuries and play activities as frivolous.
_____ 137. I hate it when someone approaches me sexually.
_____ 138. Sometimes I find children more attractive than others.
_____ 139. There are some people in my life who are hard to get over though they hurt or used me badly.
_____ 140. I feel bad when something good happens.
_____ 141. I get excited/aroused when faced with dangerous situations.
_____ 142. I use anything to distract myself from my problems.
_____ 143. Sometimes I live in an "unreal" world.
_____ 144. There are long periods of time with no sexual activity for me.

STRESS INDEX ANSWER GRID

© Copyright Patrick J. Carnes, PhD, CAS 1999

- On the answer grid below, place an "X" by all the questions that you checked as **true for you.**
- Next, add up all the Xs in each column and place the total in the space at the bottom of each column.

1	2	3	4	5	6	7	8
9	10	11	12	13	14	15	16
17	18	19	20	21	22	23	24
25	26	27	28	29	30	31	32
33	34	35	36	37	38	39	40
41	42	43	44	45	46	47	48
49	50	51	52	53	54	55	56
57	58	59	60	61	62	63	64
65	66	67	68	69	70	71	72
73	74	75	76	77	78	79	80
81	82	83	84	85	86	87	88
89	90	91	92	93	94	95	96
97	98	99	100	101	102	103	104
105	106	107	108	109	110	111	112
113	114	115	116	117	118	119	120
121	122	123	124	125	126	127	128
129	130	131	132	133	134	135	136
137	138	139	140	141	142	143	144
TRT	TR	TBD	TS	TP	TB	TSG	TA
___	___	___	___	___	___	___	___

Note: Transfer your score for each category (TRT, TR, etc.) to the appropriate section Chapter 7. You may also want to transfer your scores to the PTSI Overview that follows.

PTSI Analysis Overview
© Copyright Patrick J. Carnes, PhD, CAS 1999

Based on your scores for the Post-Traumatic Stress Index (PTSI), the following is a brief explanation of what the score measures. If you have been in recovery then these are possible "vulnerable" areas of which to be aware.

- *If your score is **low (0-2)** this is not an area of concern.*

- *If your score is **moderate (3-6)** you may wish to explore strategies that might help resolve the past or how to reduce your vulnerability in this area.*

- *If your score **is severe (7-18**) then this is an area of potential intense focus for you or an area of periodic significance.*

Obviously, the higher the number, the more concern one has about the severity and chronicity of brain change.

Please note that this screening instrument assists in beginning to think about the potential role of trauma or relational experiences in your life.

Further assessment with your therapist will determine if these results "fit" and what protocols to consider.

TRT - Trauma Reactions: My score _____

Experiencing current reactions to trauma events in the past. This relates to post-traumatic stress disorder (PTSD) symptoms and a tendency to over-react or under-react. Most individuals who score in this area experienced some kind of anxiety (stress) in their family of origin, or growing up and feeling a sense of fear or terror (lack of safety). This sense of uncertainty may be acute or chronic and longitudinal. The general idea is that perceived trauma by an individual results in the release of stress hormones, which may actually damage (rewire) the brain when stress is sustained.

Typical therapeutic strategies:

- Study and write down your automatic "knee jerk" reactions and distorted thinking.

- Write letters to those who facilitated less-than nurturing experiences for you, telling them of the long-term impact you are experiencing.

- Also write amends letters to those you know you have harmed.

- Decide with a therapist what is appropriate to send.

- You may need to wait until you are further along in your individual and coupleship (if applicable) recovery before attending to amends.

TR - Trauma Repetition: My score _____

Repeating behaviors or situations that parallel early relationally traumatic experiences. This relates to reenactment and the tendency to "do over." Individuals who score in this area often report OCD or OCPD features (hyper-focus, obsession, rumination).

Typical therapeutic strategies:

- Understand how history repeats itself in your life experiences.

- Develop habits which help to center yourself (e.g., breathing, journaling, meditation, light exercise) so you are doing what you intend -- not the cycles of old.

- Work on boundaries, both external and internal. Boundary failure is key to repetition compulsion.

TBD - Trauma Bonds: My score _____
Being connected (loyal, helpful or supportive) to people who are dangerous, shaming or exploitative. People who score in this area tend to trust those they should not and to mistrust those they should.

Typical therapeutic strategies:

- Learn to recognize trauma bonds by identifying those in your life.
- Look for patterns.
- Use "detachment" strategies in difficult situations or with people who "trigger" your codependence.

TS - Trauma Shame: My score _____
Feeling unworthy, or helpless/hopeless/worthless; having self-hate because of trauma experience. This relates to a sense of self, self-esteem and the experience of thinking "I'm not enough" and "I'm not safe" (e.g., "I can't be myself and be enough, and I'm not safe in this world ... being who I am"). Often, individuals will react to stress with extremes (under or over-functioning, grandiosity or worthlessness, over-control or helplessness and avoidance or passive-aggressive behavior, excessive neediness or hopelessness).
Typical therapeutic strategies:

- Understand shame dynamics in your family of origin and how those patterns repeat in your relationships today.
- To whom was it important that you feel ashamed?
- Write a list of your secrets.
- Begin reprogramming yourself with 10 affirmations 10 times a day (100, and in front of the mirror is best).

TP - Trauma Pleasure Neuropathway: My score _____
This is one of the addictive neuropathways related to intensity. When the brain is triggered limbically, automatic reactions ensue and defenses (familiar coping mechanisms) result. Individuals who score in this area often find pleasure in the presence of extreme danger, violence, risk or shame. Thoughts/behaviors primarily used to reduce pain and acted out with Intensity, Risk, Danger, Power/Control.

Typical therapeutic strategies:

- Write a history of how excitement and shame are linked to your trauma past.
- Note the costs and dangers to you over time.
- Write a First Step and relapse prevention plan about how powerful this is in your life.

How this neuropathway facilitates behavioral symptoms in various areas:

(1) Erotic (sexual): All focus is on erotic behavior, excitement, sexual possibility and orgasm. High intensity, risk and danger are often associated. Trauma survivors may incorporate pain and trauma into behavior. Violent/Painful S&M. Voyeuristic Rape. Humiliation. Degradation. Anonymous. Prostitutes. One-night stands. Exhibitionism. Swinging/Swapping. Massage Parlors. Adult Bookstores. Frotterism. Masturbation w/or without porn or 900#.

(2) Romance (sexual): Romance junkies turn new love into a "fix." They fall into love repeatedly or simultaneously. Roller-coaster romances are highly sexual, volatile, and dangerous. Partners are often unreachable, unavailable or unreadable. Seduction. Exploitation. Conquest. Flirtation. Fatal Attraction syndrome. Having sex with employees and professional "relationships." Office romances. Affair with neighbor. Affairs. Harassment. Swinging/Swapping. Clubs/Bars.

(3) Relationship (sexual): Volatile, intense, controlling and often dangerous relationships. Traumatic bonding, stalking and codependency thrive in abandonment, fear-based or dangerous collaborations. Cycles of sex and breakups. High involvement with a stalker. Keep trying to "break it off." Seen in public with a lover. Domestic Violence Syndrome.

(4) Drugs|Money|Food: Methamphetamine, Cocaine, Ecstasy, Violence. Craps, Race Track. Over-eating. When facilitated in Health (ability to self-soothe): Life-Enhancing, Passion, Advocacy.

TB - Trauma Blocking Neuropathway: My score _____

This is one of the addictive neuropathways related to numbing. When the brain is triggered limbically, automatic reactions ensue and defenses (familiar coping mechanisms) result. Patterns exist to numb and block out overwhelming feelings that stem from trauma in your life. The unconscious need is for satiation and trancing, which is used to soothe the anxiety and stress of daily life. Behavior is used to sleep, to calm down, or to manage internal discomfort. Anxiety occurs when highly ritualized behavior is frustrated or disturbed. Thoughts/Behaviors primarily used to reduce anxiety.

Typical therapeutic strategies:

- Work to identify experiences in which you felt pain or diminished.
- Re-experience the feelings in a safe place with the help of your therapist and make sense of them as an adult. This will reduce the power they have had in your life.
- Write a First Step if necessary.

How this neuropathway facilitates behavioral symptoms in various areas:

(1) Erotic (sexual): Sex is used to soothe the anxiety and stress of daily life. Sex is used to sleep, to calm down high-risk takers, or to manage internal discomfort. Anxiety occurs when highly ritualized behavior is frustrated or disturbed. Masturbation to sleep. Adult Bookstores. Lounges. 900#. Internet. Voyeurism.

(2) Romantic (sexual): Romance becomes a way to manage anxiety. Person becomes anxious if not in love with someone or with the person loved. How you are and who the other is not as important as the comfort of being attached. The only goal is to be with someone. Avoid being alone/lonely at all costs. Serial or simultaneous dating/ marriage. CoSA/S-Anon.

(3) Relationship (sexual): Compulsive relationships include tolerating the intolerable – battering, addiction, abuse and deprivation. Person will distort reality rather than face abandonment. Domestic Violence.

(4) Drugs/Money/Food: Alcohol, Valium, Heroin. Slot Machines. Over-eating. When facilitated in Health (ability to self-soothe): Reflective, Calming, Solitude.

TSG - Trauma Splitting Neuropathway: My score _____

This is one of the addictive neuropathways related to dissociation. Dissociation exists on a continuum from "simply spacing out sometimes when driving" to severe Dissociative Identity Disorder. When the brain is triggered limbically, automatic reactions ensue and defenses (familiar coping mechanisms) result. Ignoring traumatic realities by dissociating or compartmentalizing experiences or parts of the self. Flighting in to fantasy and unreality as an escape. Dissociation and OCD symptoms are typical. Obsession and preoccupation become the solution to painful reality. Fantasy is an escape used to procrastinate, avoid grief and ignore pain. The neurochemicals involved are typically estrogens and androgens that occur naturally for libido, lust and the drive to procreate. In terms of courtship disorder, this results in dysfunctional patterns of noticing, attraction, touching and foreplay. Thoughts/behaviors primarily used to reduce shame. Acting out with Dissociation, Compartmentalizing, Escape, Obsession.

Typical therapeutic strategies:

- Learn that dissociating is a "normal" response to trauma.
- Identify ways you split reality and the triggers that cause that to happen.
- Cultivate a "caring" adult who stays present so you can remain whole.
- Notice any powerlessness you feel and how you're drawn to control or having to know exactly what/how/why, or managing the outcome, and may experience difficulty with flexibility and trusting the process.

How this neuropathway facilitates behavioral symptoms in various areas:

(1) Erotic (sexual): Obsession and preoccupation become the solution to painful reality. Fantasy is an escape used to procrastinate, avoid grief and ignore pain. Ultimate orgasm, Strip clubs. Swinging/Swapping. Cruising. Cybersex. Porn. 900#. High ritualization.

(2) Romantic (sexual): Person avoids life problems through romantic preoccupation. Planning, intrigue and research fill the void. Emails and chats, magical romance and stalking are more real than family. Erotic Stories. Sexual misconduct. Stalking. Internet "soulmate".

(3) Relationship (sexual): Compulsive relationships are built on distorted fantasy. Charisma, role, cause, gratitude play role in cults, sexual misconduct and betrayal. Mystique is built on secrecy, belief in uniqueness, and "special" needs/wants. "Cosmic Relationship".

(4) Drugs/Money/Food: Cannabis, LSD. Internet Lottery. Binge-Purge. When facilitated in Health (ability to self-soothe): Focus(ed).

TA - Trauma Abstinence: My score _____

As a result of traumatic experience, individuals who score in this area tend to deprive (also noted as Trauma Deprivation or TD) themselves of things that are wanted, needed or deserved. There is difficulty in meeting for, or asking for help in meeting, one's needs and wants. Trauma Aversion is used to reduce terror/fear by providing a false sense of control. Often individuals will experience or act out in extremes or binge/purge patterns. Thoughts/Behaviors used primarily to reduce terror/fear. Acted out with Control and Binge-Purge.

Typical therapeutic strategies:
- Understand how deprivation is a way to continue serving your perpetrators.
- Write a letter to the victim that was you in the past and how you learned to tolerate pain and deprivation.
- Work on strategies to self-nurture and protect/comfort your inner child.
- Visualize yourself as a precious child of the universe.

How this neuropathway facilitates behavioral symptoms in various areas:
(1) Erotic (sexual): Anything erotic or suggestive is rejected. Sex is threatening, mundane, tolerable; not pleasurable. Sex may be okay if the other person does not matter (objectified). Self-mutilation. Objectification of self, being used (prostitution).

(2) Romantic (sexual): Extreme distrust of romantic feelings or initiatives. At best person seeks "arrangement." Marriage without sex. Suspicious of kindness (seeks ulterior motives). Avoid and withdraw.

(3) Relationship (sexual): Avoids. Isolated, lonely, restricted emotions and poor or nonexistent communication skills. May be overly intellectual/analytical. Secret attachments (nobody can know that I care about …)

(4) Drugs/Money/Food: Under-earning, Hoarding. When facilitated in Health (ability to self-soothe): Ascetic (for a higher purpose – as in choosing celibacy as a spiritual way of life, or abstinence for a specific period of time to promote self-awareness and healthy nurturing).

Endnotes for *Behind the Mask: Authentic Living for Young Women*

Chapter 1

[1] Centers for Disease Control and Prevention, Youth Risk Behavior Surveillance---United States , 1995, "Morbidity and Morality Weekly Report: Surveillance Summary," 46, no. 6 (November 14, 1997):1-56.

[2] Laura Sessions Stepp, Washington Post Staff writer. "The Washington Post Study: Half of All Tend to Have Had Oral Sex," Washington Post, Friday, September 16, 2005.

[3] Patrick Carnes, "Old Temptation, New Technology: Pornography and Internet in Today's World," Enrichment (Fall 2005): 22-29.

[4] Centers for Disease Control and Prevention, Youth Risk Behavior Surveillance---United States , 1995, "Morbidity and Morality Weekly Report: Surveillance Summary," 46, no. 6 (November 14, 1997):1-56.

Chapter 2

[5] An online survey conducted by TRU, a global leader in research on teens and 20-somethings, conducted between September 25, 2008 and October 3, 2008. For additional data visit www.TheNationalCampaignog/sextech or contact The National Campaign at 202.478.8500

[6] Ibid.

[7] ibid.

[8] Cleon Rogers Jr. & Cleon Rogers III, *The New Linguistic and Exegetical Key to the Greek New Testament* (Grand Rapids, Michigan: Zondervan, 1998) 339.

[9] Adapted from Diane Roberts, *Accept No Substitutes* (Gresham, OR: Pure Desire Ministries International, 1995) 23.

Chapter 3

[10] Patrick J. Carnes. © 2008, P. J. Carnes, Sexual Addiction Screening Test – Revised. Test & Scoring information used by permission.

[11] Ted Roberts, *Pure Desire: Seven Pillars of Freedom* (Gresham, OR: Pure Desire Ministries International, 2009) 56.

[12] CDC, HIV in the United States Fact Sheet, www.cdc.gov/hiv/resources/factsheets/us.htm. November 2011.

[13] CDC, Genial HPV infection Fact Sheet, www.cdc.gov/std/HPV/STD-Fact-HPV.htm. July 22,2010.

[14] CDC, Genial HPV Fact Sheet, www.cdc.gov/STD/herpes/Herpes-Fact-Sheet.pdf. Update December 2007, July 22, 2010.

[15] CDC: Hepatitis B Fact Sheet, www.cdc.gov/ncidod/diseases/hepatitis/b/bfact.pdf. July 2007 & CDC: Hepatitis C Fact Sheet, www.cdc.gov/ncidod/diseases/hepatitis/c/cfact.pdf. March 2008.

[16] CDC, Trichomoniasis Fact Sheet, www.cdc.gov/std/Trichomonas/STDFact-Trichomoniasis.htm October 6, 2010.

[17] Chlamydia-CDC Fact Sheet. www.cdc.gov/std/chiamydia/STDFact-Chlamydia.htm. Updated May 2010.

[18] Gonorrhea-CDC Fact Sheet. www.cdc.gov/std/Gonorrhea/STDFact-gonorrhea.htm. Updated December 2007. Printed online July 22, 2010

[19] Syphilis-CDC Fact Sheet. www.cdc.gov/std/syphilis/STDFact-Syphilis.htm. Updated December 2007. Printed online July 2010.

[20] CDC-Sexually Transmitted Diseases Suveillance,2008 http://www.cdc.gov/std/stts08/trends.htm

[21] *Fireproof Magazine*, Pasadena, CA: fireproofministries.com <http://fireproofministries.com>, Fall Issue 2011) 4-5.

[22] Joe S. Mcilhaney, Jr.MD. and Freda McKissic Bush. MD. *Hooked, New Science on How Casual Sex is Affecting our Children,* Northfield Publishing, Chicago, IL , 2008, p. 111.

[23] Louis Cozolino, *The Neuroscience of Human Relationships* (New York: W.W. Norton & Company, 2006) 304.

[24] Patrick Carnes, *Facing the Shadow* (Carefree, Arizona: Gentle Path Press, 2005) 91.

[25] Ted Roberts, *Seven Pillars of Freedom* (Gresham, OR: Pure Desire Ministries International, 2009) 62.

[26] Diane Roberts, *Pure Desire for Women: Eight Pillars of Freedom from Love Addiction & Sexual Issues,* Book 1, (Gresham, OR: Pure Desire Ministries International, (2010) 77.

Chapter 4

[27] Adapted from Ted Roberts & Bryan Roberts, *Top Gun: Flight Manual for Young Men in a Pornified World* (Gresham, OR: Pure Desire Ministries International, 2011), Chapter 5.

[28] Striof, Bob. "Teen Marriage: History, Statistics, Things to Consider." About.com. 15 November 2008 http://marriage.about.com/cs/teenarriage/a/teenmarriage_2.htm

[29] Joe S. McIlhaney Jr, MD and Freda McKissic Bush, MD, *Hooked, New Science on How Casual Sex is Affecting our Children*, (Chicago: Northfield Publishing, 2008) 16.

[30] Helen Fisher, "Lust, Attraction, Attachment: Biology and Evolution of the Three Primary Emotion Systems for Mating, Reproduction, and Parenting." Journal of Sex Education and Therapy, Vol. 25, No. 1, 2000 pg. 96-104.

[31] Adapted from Ted Roberts & Bryan Roberts, *Top Gun: Flight Manual for Young Men in a Pornified World* (Gresham, OR: Pure Desire Ministries International, 2011), Chapter 5.

[32] Louann Bizendine, M.D. *The Female Brain* (New York: Broadway Books, 2006) 33.

[33] Ibid. 37.

[34] Adapted from Ted Roberts & Bryan Roberts, *Top Gun: Flight Manual for Young Men in a Pornified World* (Gresham, OR: Pure Desire Ministries International, 2011), Chapter 5.

[35] Sharon Begley, *"Train Your Mind Change Your Brain,"* (New York: Ballantine Books, 2008) 9-25.

[36] Content & exercises for portions of *Behind the Mask* Chapter 4 have been adapted from the work of Ted Roberts, Pure Desire Ministries International, Gresham, OR. Used by permission.

[37] Ted Roberts, *Pure Desire: Seven Pillars of Freedom* (Gresham, Oregon: Pure Desire Ministries , International, 2009) 111-118.

[38] Ibid. 115.

[39] Markus Barth, *Ephesians 4-6* (New York: Doubleday, 1974) 777.

Chapter 5

[40] Edward Laumann, Robert T. Michael and Gina Kolata, *Sex in America* (New York: Time Warner,1995) 127.

[41] Joe S. Mcilhaney, Jr. MD., Freda Mckissic Bush, MD., *Hooked, New Science on How Casual Sex is Affecting our Children.* (Chicago: Northfield Publishing, 2008) 133.

[42] Brennan Manning, *The ragamuffin Gospel* (Colorado Springs, CO: Multnomah Books, 2005) 171-172.

[43] Philip Yancey, *Disappointment with God,* (New York: Harper Collins Publishers, 1988) 215-217.

[44] John Demos, *Neurofeedback,* (New York: W.W. Norton, 2005) 22-56.

[45] John Ratey, *A User's Guide to the Brain,* (New York: Vintage Books: 2001) 227.

[46] Michael Dye, *The Genesis Process for Change Groups, Book Two* (Auburn, CA: Michael Dye, 2006) www.genesisprocess.org

[47] Diane Roberts. *Betrayal and Beyond* (Gresham, OR: Pure Desire Ministries International, 2010) adaptation & summary of pp. 95-111, most of which was contributed by Jane Carter.

[48] Michael Dye, *The Genesis Process for Change Groups, Book One* (Auburn, CA: Michael Dye, 2006) 45. www.genesisprocess.org

Chapter 6

[49] Bill Thrall, Bruce McNicol, and John Lynch, *TrueFaced, Trust God and Others with Who You Really Are*, Revised Edition (Colorado Springs: Navpress,2004) 70.

[50] Ted Roberts, Pure Desire: Seven Pillars (Gresham, OR: Pure Desire Ministries International, 2009) 161-164.

Chapter 7

[51] Post Traumatic Stress Index Test & Analysis. Copyright Patrick J. Carnes, PhD,CAS 1999. Used by permission of Patrick J. Carnes. The PTSI and the evaluation terminology are based Dr. Carnes' work.

[52] Ted Roberts, *Pure Desire, Seven Pillars of Freedom Men's Workbook*, (Gresham, Oregon: Pure Desire Ministries, International, 2009). 235-248. Some of the text was adapted for use in *Pure Desire For Women*.

[53] Patrick Carnes, *The Betrayal Bond: Breaking Free of Exploitive Relationships,* (Deerfield Beach, Florida: Health Communications, Inc. 1997), pg. 114.

[54] Ibid. 34-35.

[55] Michael Dye, *The Genesis Process for Change Groups, Book Two*, (Auburn, CA: Michael Dye, 2006) 59-61. www.genesisprocess.org.

Chapter 8

[56] Ted Roberts, *Pure Desire, Seven Pillars to Freedom*, (Gresham, Oregon: Pure Desire Ministries, International: 2009), Lesson teaching is adapted from Pillar 6.

Chapter 9

[57] Ted Roberts, *For Men Only* (Gresham, Oregon: East Hill Church, 1993) 26-27.

[58] Covenant Eyes booklet, *Parenting the Internet Generation* (Owosso, MI: Covenant Eyes, 2010) 6.

[59] Daniel Siegel, MD, *Mind Sight, The New Science of Personal Transformation,* (New York: Bantam Books/Random House Inc., 2010) 55.

Chapter 10

[60] The section on fantasy has been summarized & adapted & from Ted Roberts, *Pure Desire, Seven Pillars of Freedom Men's Workbook*, (Gresham, Oregon: Pure Desire Ministries, International, 2009). 182-185.

[61] JK Rowling. *Harry Potter and the Sorcerer' Stone.* (New York: Arthur A Levine Books, 1999)

[62] The concept of the Mirror of Erised comes from the sexual addiction therapist training Ted Roberts received through IITAP. www.IITAP.com

Chapter 11

[63] Ted Roberts, *Pure Desire, Seven Pillars to Freedom*, (Gresham, Oregon: Pure Desire Ministries, International: 2009)John 8 teaching is adapted from page 19.

[64] The Three Circles exercise used here is an adaptation of the Three Circles used by Sex Addicts Anonymous. The original is available through Sex Addicts Anonymous and pamphlets available online through the SAA Store or by telephone or postal mail from the ISO office. www.sexaa.org

[65] The Three Circles exercise used here is an adaptation of the Three Circles used by Sex Addicts Anonymous. The original is available through Sex Addicts Anonymous and pamphlets available online through the SAA Store or by telephone or postal mail from the ISO office. www.sexaa.org

Chapter 12

[66] Henry Cloud and John Townsend, *Boundaries*, (Grand Rapids, Michigan: Zondervan, 1992) 32.

[67] Merie A. Fossum and Marilyn J. Mason, *Facing Shame*, (New York: W.W. Norton & Co., 1986) 70-71.

[68] Byron Kehler, Agape Youth and Family Ministries, concept taken from "Self-Care" Handout, Milwaukie, Oregon, 1992.

[69] Braun-Courville,D.K.,& Rohas, M. "Exposure to Sexually Explicit Web Sites and Adolescent Sexual Attitudes and Behaviors," *Journal of Adolescent Health* 38 (2006) 433-47.

[70] Guilamo-Ramos, V. & Bouris, A, "Working with Parents to Promote Healthy Adolescent Sexual Development," The Prevention Researcher, Vol. 16, No. 4 (2009): 7-119.

[71] Dating plan is adapted from Dr. Ted Roberts & Bryan Roberts, *Top Gun* (Gresham, OR: Pure Desire Ministries International, 2011) pp. 121-122.

Chapter 13

[72] Diane Roberts, *Betrayal & Beyond Book 3*, (Gresham, OR: Pure Desire Ministries International, 2010) Chapter 13 is adapted from Pillar Seven, Lesson Two, "Unhealthy Anger," written by Elizabeth Drago & Teri Vietti.

[73] Wanda Fisher, "Anger Test" (Eugene, Oregon: Faith Center). Used by permission of Wanda Fisher.

[74] Wanda Fisher, "Repressed or Explosive Anger" (Eugene, Oregon: Faith Center). Used by permission of Wanda Fisher.

[75] Diane Roberts, *Pure Desire for Women: Eight Pillars to Freedom from Love Addiction & Sexual Issues, Book 2*, (Gresham, OR: Pure Desire Ministries International, 2010) Adapted from Pillar Eight, Lesson Three, written by Teri Vietti.

[76] Laurie Hall, *An Affair of the Mind*, (Wheaton, Illinois: Tyndale House, 1996) 218.

[77] RT Kendall, *Total Forgiveness*, (Lake Mary, Florida: Florida Charisma House, 2002) XXXIII.

Chapter 15

[78] Ted Roberts, *The Popeye Problem*, idea adapted from a sermon presented at East Hill Church, Gresham, OR, 2011.

[79] Henry Cloud and John Townsend, *Safe People*, (Grand Rapids, MI: Zondervan, 1995) summary of 189-199.

[80] Ibid Summery of 27-38.

[81] J.R.R. Tolkien, Lord of the Rings, (New York: Houghton Mifflin).

[82] Alfred Ells, *One-Way Relationships*, (Nashville, TN: Nelson Publisher,1990) 189-193.

[83] Taylor-Johnson Temperament Analysis. The T-JTA is a widely used personality assessment for individual, marital, premarital, and family counseling. The T-JTA measures 18 dimensions of personality (9 bipolar traits) that are important components of personal adjustment and in interpersonal relationships. www.tjta.com/

Resources

[84] Ted Roberts. Adapted from *Living Life Boldly Study Guide,* (Gresham, OR: East Hill Church, 2005) 75-76. Used by permission.

[85] Post Traumatic Stress Index Test & Analysis. Copyright Patrick J. Carnes, PhD,CAS 1999. Used by permission of Patrick J. Carnes.